THE
BOOK
OF
HAPPY

250 WAYS TO
A HAPPIER YOU

Adams Media
New York   London   Toronto   Sydney   New Delhi

Adams Media
An Imprint of Simon & Schuster, Inc.
57 Littlefield Street
Avon, Massachusetts 02322

Copyright © 2018 by Simon & Schuster, Inc.

All rights reserved, including the right to reproduce this book or portions thereof in any form whatsoever. For information address Adams Media Subsidiary Rights Department, 1230 Avenue of the Americas, New York, NY 10020.

First Adams Media trade paperback edition December 2018

ADAMS MEDIA and colophon are trademarks of Simon & Schuster.

For information about special discounts for bulk purchases, please contact Simon & Schuster Special Sales at 1-866-506-1949 or business@simonandschuster.com.

The Simon & Schuster Speakers Bureau can bring authors to your live event. For more information or to book an event contact the Simon & Schuster Speakers Bureau at 1-866-248-3049 or visit our website at www.simonspeakers.com.

Interior design by Erin Alexander

Manufactured in the United States of America

10 9 8 7 6 5 4 3 2 1

Library of Congress Cataloging-in-Publication Data has been applied for.

ISBN 978-1-5072-1007-9
ISBN 978-1-5072-1008-6 (ebook)

Many of the designations used by manufacturers and sellers to distinguish their products are claimed as trademarks. Where those designations appear in this book and Simon & Schuster, Inc., was aware of a trademark claim, the designations have been printed with initial capital letters.

This book is intended as general information only, and should not be used to diagnose or treat any health condition. In light of the complex, individual, and specific nature of health problems, this book is not intended to replace professional medical advice. The ideas, procedures, and suggestions in this book are intended to supplement, not replace, the advice of a trained medical professional. Consult your physician before adopting any of the suggestions in this book, as well as about any condition that may require diagnosis or medical attention. The author and publisher disclaim any liability arising directly or indirectly from the use of this book.

Contains material adapted from the following titles published by Adams Media, an Imprint of Simon & Schuster, Inc.: *Mantras Made Easy* by Sherianna Boyle, MEd, CAGS, copyright © 2017, ISBN 978-1-4405-9997-2; *Happiness Hacks* by Adams Media, copyright © 2018, ISBN 978-1-5072-0634-8; *Rituals for Life* by Meera Lester, copyright © 2017, ISBN 978-1-5072-0524-2; *Quotes to Live By* by Adams Media, copyright © 2013, ISBN 978-1-4405-6088-0; *Stress Less* by Kate Hanley, copyright © 2017, ISBN 978-1-5072-0193-0; *My Pocket Meditations* by Meera Lester, copyright © 2017, ISBN 978-1-5072-0341-5; *365 Ways to Live Happy* by Meera Lester, copyright © 2010, ISBN 978-1-60550-028-7; *My Pocket Guru* by Adams Media, copyright © 2016, ISBN 978-1-4405-9246-1; *The Little Book of Self-Care* by Adams Media, copyright © 2017, ISBN 978-1-5072-0491-7; *Meditation Made Easy* by Preston Bentley, copyright © 2015, ISBN 978-1-4405-8432-9.

Introduction

Everybody wants to be happy, right? It's something that most people on earth seem to be searching for. In today's chaotic society, though, it can be tough to find joy when there's so much wrong with the world. But not for you! That's because you've picked up *The Book of Happy* to help you find the small things in life that make every day a little more wonderful.

Throughout the book you'll find 250 different ways to bring joy, laughter, and happiness directly into your life, including:

- Daily rituals
- Happiness hacks
- Inspirational quotes
- Relaxation techniques
- Empowering mantras
- And more…

From learning to say no to simply smiling more, the ideas in this book will give you the tools to live the happiest, most blissful life you can, whether you're frustrated at work, upset over the struggles in the world, or just need a pick-me-up after a particularly tough day.

If you struggle to find a spark of joy in the midst of your life, don't worry. *The Book of Happy* has just what you need to perk up and see the brighter side of things again—anytime you need it.

◆

There is no path to happiness: happiness is the path.

—GAUTAMA BUDDHA
Sixth-century spiritual leader and founder of Buddhism

Gaze at a Gorgeous You

Put a picture of yourself from a happy time in your life on your desk. Gaze at an image of yourself looking fabulous. Find a photo of yourself taken when you felt most alive, then frame it and put it where you can easily see it. Looking at positive images of yourself can push aside a mountain of negative thoughts, boost your self-esteem, and make you feel good. What if none of your photos are that great? No problem. Use digital image tools to rework a scanned photo or digital image: erase some of those wrinkles, add some hair, shift some curves, and turn back the clock. Have fun creating a fabulous-looking new you! Then look at the photo whenever you need a little dose of happiness and let it spark some good vibes.

✦

The key to being
happy is knowing
you have the
power to choose
what to accept and
what to let go.

—DODINSKY
American author

Be Grateful for All You Have

Make gratitude a guiding principle of your life. Start by practicing mindfulness in the present moment. Let your senses of sight, smell, hearing, taste, and touch and your intuition inform you of the great power and blessing inherent in a single moment. Absorbed, you let go of doing and come into being. Joy rises spontaneously in you but because you are so focused you might not realize how happy and satisfied you feel. Even more marvelous is that you lose your sense of individuality and worries fall away. To be able to practice mindfulness is itself a gift. This ancient practice can lead you to appreciate the interconnectedness of all life and a desire to acknowledge all the goodness that exists in every single moment. In turn, such feelings of gratitude for how you are blessed can trigger a desire to help others find happiness.

Try using a small stone with the word *gratitude* printed on it as a touchstone to remind you to use positive language and say thank you often. Carry it in your pocket so that throughout the day whenever you touch it, you'll be reminded to sow seeds of gratitude.

Tell Yourself You're Happy

This mantra reminds you that you get to choose what you're aligned with: either happiness or fear. To align yourself more closely and consistently with happiness, simply call upon your imagination and repeat the mantra, *I align myself with happiness.*

According to Albert Einstein, "Imagination is more important than knowledge." This is because when it comes to your body, reality and fantasy tend to overlap. If you imagine you are feeling happy and content, your body picks up on this and creates the experience for you. The powerful benefits of visualization are supported by neuroscience. Much of being happy really is all in your mind.

✦

The purpose of life is to be happy.

—TENZIN GYATSO
His Holiness the fourteenth Dalai Lama

Eat Chocolate

When you want a moment of pure pleasure, eat some dark chocolate. Not only does it make you feel good, it has specific health benefits, namely that dark chocolate increases the brain's serotonin and endorphin levels. In other words, it enhances your feelings of pleasure and happiness. Dark chocolate can also lower high blood pressure and improve blood flow through arteries and veins. It's a powerful antioxidant too. See? Chocolate is the perfect food! Just nibbling a little piece of chocolate can lift your spirits *and* it's good for you.

Make Meditation Delicious

"Mindful eating" can sound a bit wholesome and boring, but slowing down and paying attention enhances the pleasure of the experience. Why not give it a try? Start with something super easy—like meditatively eating a piece of chocolate! To do it, hold the chocolate in your hand. Feel its weight. Think of all the people involved in growing, picking, processing, and shipping the beans, turning the beans into chocolate, and shipping the chocolate to your store. Thank them.

Now savor every facet of eating a tiny bite—the smell, the taste, the physiological response you feel in your body. Keep giving your full attention to the act of eating until the chocolate is gone. What did you notice?

Acknowledge Your Blessings

To say that you are blessed is far more than saying you have good luck or fortune. Acknowledge your blessings simply by repeating *I am blessed* to yourself. To be blessed is to be aware that you are holy and therefore have received grace. It is important to keep this in mind as you recite this mantra. Mindfulness allows you to be grateful for who you are right now, rather than who you hope to be, and can bring a calm happiness into your life.

Another version of this mantra is *We are blessed*. This statement gives you the ability to see and honor the grace in others as well.

✦

You know what
I really need?...
Absolutely nothing.
I don't need a
thing in the world.
I am the happiest
man on the face
of the earth.

—FATHER MYCHAL JUDGE
New York City Fire Department chaplain

Look for the Good in a Bad Situation

Every one of us has experienced losses—some more extreme than others—but there is often a seed of triumph hidden in those losses. It may be hard to see at first, but it's there. Try asking yourself: *What is the good in this? What lesson can I take away? How can I share my knowledge with others?* Bring to mind two or three events that may have seemed totally awful up to this point and write down only the good things and/or the benefits gained from each. Looking for the brighter side is a great habit to develop—you'll become a happier and more compassionate person.

Gain a Calm Mind and Joy with Meditation

A calm, healthy mind can actually bring about noticeable physiological changes to your body. Slower breathing drives down blood pressure and heart rate. As your oxygen consumption goes down, your mind—in a state of relaxed awareness—begins to behold itself and experience joy. This is the foundation for the meditation and contemplation practiced by saints and sages over time throughout the world and can bring you a joyful peace.

1. With eyes closed, direct your attention to the space between your brows. This will be your focal point for this meditation. Gently gaze into that space without straining.
2. As thoughts or emotions arise to threaten your peace, don't try to reason, deny, or argue them away. That would be conflicting and counterproductive, derailing your meditation. Don't be hard on yourself but rather practice patience and loving-kindness.
3. Maintain a detached awareness of what arises during meditation.

In Buddhism, inner peace isn't a static condition. It's a dynamic state brimming with insight, perception, knowledge, and compassion. Hold on to the awareness of that inner peace. Carry that joyful serenity unhindered into your day.

Prioritize Yourself

When you're feeling overwhelmed by a large number of responsibilities and priorities, repeat this mantra to bring happiness into your life: *I give myself permission to prioritize the things that bring me joy, creativity, and connection.* At times, you might lose your sense of direction or wonder if your life choices are off base. For example, you may crave a different lifestyle or a compatible companion. This mantra reminds you that perhaps these doubts mean that you are being connected to your divine purpose. Your creative energy can stimulate healthy change and lead to happy experiences. So allow yourself to feel these doubts, and ask yourself if they could become motivation for you to reclaim happiness. Rather than focusing on what is missing from your life, this mantra encourages you to incorporate things that bring you joy (e.g., animals, nature, art, music, etc.).

✦

Now and then
it's good to
pause in our
pursuit of
happiness and
just be happy.

—GUILLAUME APOLLINAIRE
French poet

Put On a Happy Face

Sometimes when it comes to feeling happy, you have to fake it 'til you make it, so force yourself to smile. Now hold that smile for a count of ten. Think to yourself, *I am happy. I am totally, blissfully happy.* You'll notice that your mood will begin to shift. You can't help but feel a little lighter. Use your smile to start a happiness epidemic! Smile at everyone, everywhere. People are hardwired to respond to the facial expressions they encounter. If you glower at someone, that person will return a frown, but if you smile, you'll get a smile back. You'll feel happier, too, because your body will respond to your smile even if you are faking the grin. So go ahead—fake it until you genuinely feel happy!

Create a Vision Board

Depict the abundance you desire. Your words, thoughts, emotions, and mental images—all have a potential to shift your life in a different direction. You might have heard of or even created a vision board to solidify ideas for a project or something you wanted to focus on with intensity. For this vision board, take a large piece of poster board and draw three rows of three boxes each (nine equal boxes). Starting at the bottom, label the boxes left to right as *knowledge*, *career*, and *helpful people*. Next row up, label the boxes left to right as *health*, *balance*, and *creativity*. And on the top row, also left to right, label the boxes *money*, *fame*, and *love*. Cut and paste images that reflect for you abundance relative to each box. The idea is to create a vision for the life you want with a belief that what you can see, you can manifest.

Put your vision board next to your desk. Each morning or night (or both), hold the board and study the boxes, adding other images to them as you're inspired. Feel happy and excited and worthy. Trust that what you see you are going to get. State the affirmation: *I welcome abundance that flows easily to me for every sector of my life. May every living being and creature receive abundantly from the universe.*

Spread Happiness

Happiness in your life doesn't have to be purely internal. You can find great joy through making other people happy. Simple acts of kindness, such as holding the door for someone, letting someone go ahead of you in line, or paying for another person's cup of coffee are ways to spread happiness. Happiness is contagious. You can literally change the climate of a room through acts of kindness.

After you help someone, repeat the following phrase: *Appreciation and gratitude pulsate through me now.* As you recite this mantra, notice how the energy of the words rests on your heart. Breathe deeply as you send loving thoughts to yourself and the world around you.

✦

Trees are happy for no reason.

—OSHO
Indian religious leader and mystic

Exercise in the Park

If you like stretching, walking, or running, do it in nature—for example, consider joining a group of people who congregate in a nearby park to practice tai chi, qigong, or yoga. Doctors say the best kind of exercise is the kind that you enjoy enough to keep doing consistently. If you like to socialize while working out, meet some friends at a high school football field, on a jogging trail, or at a local park. Breathe some fresh air, take in the lovely sights and sounds of nature, and work out while enjoying the camaraderie of others.

Tap Into Thoreau's Tonic of Wilderness

Henry David Thoreau believed the cure for all that ails the world and the individual could be found in nature. For Thoreau, spending time in the woods in New England provided a kind of peacefulness that could center and ground him like perhaps nothing else.

You don't have to take along a bateau (a type of boat Thoreau used) or even a tent and backpack if you don't plan to stay in the wild place of your choice. The important thing is to find some place in nature where you feel centered and connected with the earth's energies. Nature will ground you when you leave behind the fast-paced world for a while. In the country or mountains or desert, time seems to slow down to a more natural rhythm. Sit and be mindful of all that your senses take in. Drink water. Roll up your pant legs; take off your shoes and socks. Run the bottoms of your feet over smooth stones or chill out in sparkling cold stream water. Let the subtle earth currents fill you with the tonic of wilderness. Feel grounded and be happy.

Attain Natural Bliss

Nature blooms all around you and can grant you immense happiness if you allow it to. When you're out in nature, say to yourself the mantra, *I receive fully the joy and nourishment nature brings*; this will help your brain produce some "happy chemicals" like serotonin and dopamine. Mantras not only support the production of these chemicals; they also shift your brain waves into more calming states. A March 2014 article in *Psychology Today* noted that "nature relatedness often predicts happiness regardless of other psychological factors." This mantra is great for those times of day when you are transitioning from indoors to outdoors (e.g., checking your mail or walking to your car). It encourages you to fully soak in the ample benefits nature provides.

✦

Folks are
usually about
as happy as
they make their
minds up to be.

—ABRAHAM LINCOLN
Sixteenth president of the United States

Choose to Think Happy Thoughts

If you want to find happiness and add years to your life, think happy thoughts. When you choose positive thoughts over negative ones, you are more likely to develop an optimistic outlook on life. According to happiness researchers such as Martin E.P. Seligman, director of the Positive Psychology Center at the University of Pennsylvania, and Barbara Fredrickson, professor of psychology at the University of North Carolina at Chapel Hill, positive people generally have higher levels of optimism and life satisfaction and live longer. In a BBC News report, Dr. Seligman said that "we have compelling evidence that optimists and pessimists will differ markedly in how long they live." Dr. Fredrickson has counseled that changing your mind-set can change your body chemistry. She has stated that positive feelings literally can open the heart and mind.

And there's more good news. Even if you aren't normally a happy person, thinking happy thoughts is a skill that can be learned. Work on being open, being an optimist, choosing to think positive thoughts, and seeing the proverbial glass half full rather than half empty. The next time you are in line at the post office and someone cuts in front of you or says something rude, resist the urge to respond with anger, which can clamp down your blood vessels and increase your blood pressure. Instead, return rudeness with kindness and respect. Keep that positive vibe going through your intentions and actions in whatever you do. The more frequently you choose to be happy, the more your effort will be strengthened. So don't fret; be happy and live longer.

Trick Your Brain Into Happiness

There's a way you can trick your mind into reliving a happy event as if it's actually happening again. Simply draw a picture in your mind of a past happy event. Use sensory details to make it come alive in your mind, creating a tangible feeling of happy anticipation. Now slowly bring yourself back to the present by becoming re-centered in your body, from the soles of your feet to the crown of your head. Take a deep breath and slowly open your eyes. You will likely feel rejuvenated and happy, ready to focus on thinking happy thoughts. This process can spark existing neurons and strengthen neural connections associated with the original memory, essentially doubling your levels of pleasure and happiness. The more you remember happy times, the happier your outlook on life will become.

Enjoy Your Experiences

Happiness and joy are experiences. Research shows that individuals who prioritize experiences over purchases tend to be happier. Think about your experiences and enjoy them in your mind as you say, *Energy flows where attention goes. I choose to focus on bliss.*

Before reciting this mantra, take a moment to close your eyes and soften the muscles in your face and shoulders. Ask your body what brings it joy. Pause and notice what comes up for you. Perhaps you'll imagine a place you like to visit, certain people in your life, listening to music, or spending time in nature. Visualize these things as you recite this mantra several times.

There's nothing like deep breaths after laughing that hard. Nothing in the world like a sore stomach for the right reasons.

—STEPHEN CHBOSKY
American author

Laugh—A Lot

Laughing is the cure for what ails you. Laughing has amazing benefits, including beating back a tide of stress hormones (cortisol, in particular), giving your body a healthy break, lowering your blood pressure, strengthening your immune system, and generating the release of endorphins (those wonderful happiness hormones). Laughter also provides a physical and emotional release, making you feel cleansed afterward. And it's a great internal workout for your body!

Write a Blessings List

Laughter, love, health, friends, family, money, spiritual growth, and a loving and powerful support network represent a cornucopia of blessings that suggest a prosperous and joyful life. In the fast-paced work environments that characterize the modern world, you might not realize how blessed you are. Almost every culture has rituals and symbols to draw abundance. An Eastern tradition is to hang in the northeast corner of a home or business a yantra (or mystical diagram) representing Lakshmi, the Hindu goddess of wealth, or Shree Kubera, mentioned in the Vedas as the ruler of wealth and riches. The northeast corner is also known as Eshaan corner, a highly energized space for worship.

Inside a red envelope, write a list of your blessings. Insert a dollar. Close the envelope and rub it between your palms to generate positive energy that will attract more of the same. Place the envelope in the northeast corner of your sacred space. Intensify the energy by placing a crystal on top of the envelope and cover both with a red cloth. Each week during the year, open the envelope, review, and add blessings to your list. Shake the dollar and the red cloth, and reassemble as before as you recite: *I attract an abundance of all good things that bless me and mine.*

Bring Joy Through Smiling

People smile because they're happy, but you can also become happy because you are smiling. Smiling (even if you fake it) can improve your mood, which makes it a lot easier to generate happy thoughts. Remind yourself of this by repeating, *I smile big, even when no one is looking.*

If you are wondering how this works, try checking yourself out while smiling in the mirror. When you smile, your eyes light up. Now notice the difference when a flat expression is on your face. Even if you don't feel much like smiling today, try getting out in the world and taking a look around. Watching children or animals or sitting in nature has a wonderful way of bringing a smile to your face. Some happy thoughts might just follow.

✦

The most
important thing
is to enjoy your life—
to be happy—
it's all that matters.

—AUDREY HEPBURN
American actress

Be Grateful

When you focus on what you love about your life, your positive emotional brain fires up. This creates a focused, positive feeling free of worry and fear, a state of mind that allows you to truly enjoy moments of happiness. Before you go to sleep each night, write down at least five things you're grateful for and pause to re-experience the pleasure each one brings you. Focus on what is making you feel lucky and good about your life, and you'll soon find that you feel more positive in general and that you begin to slow down and savor the good times.

Cultivate a Sense of Purpose

If you are someone who feels you are not on purpose with your life, do something about it. Make yourself happier. Living on purpose gives your life meaning. Some people walk through their lives half asleep, dreaming of the past, worrying about the future, missing the opportunities in each moment to be alert and aware and in tune with what they believe is their destiny. When you wake up to your life and follow your passion, you feel intensely alive. That sense of vitality translates to better health and well-being. Your self-esteem is strengthened and you have increased resilience in the face of challenges and difficulties.

Create a space in your home or workplace where you can retreat from the world. Go there often to sit—tailbone to floor pillow, yoga mat, or chair seat—in an unhurried silence.

- Let tranquility wash over you.
- Listen deeply to inner guidance (intuitive thoughts relayed from your Higher Self).
- Meditate on whatever it is you are meant to do and be.
- Spend time in your space to creatively imagine your purposeful life.

Differentiate Feelings and Experiences

Happiness is a feeling that makes you feel lighthearted and allows you to experience pleasure. Like other emotions, happiness can have a range. On one end, you can be elevated, perhaps giddy, while on the other end, you may feel quietly content. One is not better than the other; both are experiences of happiness. Joy tends to be less dependent on situations or circumstances. Joy is a state of being. Sure, you might have moments where you feel sad or even angry, but those emotions do not destroy your overall joy for living. Both are vitally important to your overall well-being. Remind yourself of this by saying, *Happiness is a feeling; joy is an experience. I choose both.*

✦

Happiness is a warm puppy.

—CHARLES M. SCHULZ
American cartoonist

Play with a Pet

Play with your pets! Take your dog for a walk or play with your cat for a few minutes each day. Feel the unconditional love and joy you can get from an animal. The act of caring and providing for a pet can give you satisfaction too. Pets require constant care and attention, and being able to give your pet that support can make you feel accomplished. Don't have a pet? Stop an owner on the street and ask to pet their dog, or watch pet videos online. A recent study found that just watching cat videos online can boost a person's energy and increase feelings of happiness.

Focus On What's Right Here

Quick, name three things that are going on right in this moment. Perhaps you're sitting some place comfortable, the sun is shining, and your pet is curled up nearby. This is an exercise you can do anytime you notice your stress levels rising, because allowing yourself to see what's right in front of you, right now, helps keep you grounded in this moment. And what a relief that is!

Speak to Your Soul

So many people try to be a happy human. Fair enough. But try to focus on being a happy soul instead by repeating, *I am a happy soul.*

Happy souls have no problem asking for guidance and support. Unhappy souls feel alone, unsupported, and disconnected. The next time you feel unsure about what to do, rather than ask your brain, ask your soul: *Soul, what would you have me do?* Your soul speaks to you through a hunch or a feeling, sometimes even visually or auditorily. Embrace each as a message guiding you toward a happy life.

✦

Let us be grateful
to the people who
make us happy; they
are the charming
gardeners who make
our souls blossom.

—MARCEL PROUST
French author

Sniff Some Lavender

Whenever you have a bad day, feel exasperated, or struggle to get out of a foul mood, sniff some lavender to restore your serenity. It's easy to see why lavender is one of the most popular scents in aromatherapy. (Scents like citrus, rose, and sandalwood are also pleasant. When you smell them, they can trigger particular memories or experiences because your olfactory nerve carries their scent straight to your brain.) There are many ways to enjoy lavender: use freshly crushed flowers set out in a bowl, set some reeds in a diffuser pot with a splash of lavender essential oil, light some lavender-scented candles, simmer lavender potpourri, or put out sachets of dried lavender. Allow the scent to lift your mood and remember that you never again have to relive a bad day.

Write a Haiku

A haiku is a three-line poem that many people use as a meditation aid. They can also just be a lot of fun to compose and bring joy to both the writer and reader. The first line is always five syllables, the second line is seven, and the last line is five again.

- To write a haiku in English, concentrate more on simply capturing a fleeting moment, evoking a beautiful image of the ephemeral quality of life.
- A haiku often focuses on a moment in nature, and typically includes a word that lets the reader know what season it is. For example, the word *daffodils* would indicate spring.
- It's traditional in Japanese haiku to use a *kireji*, or a cutting word. This word is used to show juxtaposition between two ideas in the haiku, or to signal the end of one of the images. In English, it's typically done with a punctuation mark, like a dash or period, since our language works differently.
- Read your haiku to family and friends. Post them around your office at work or in your home. Use them as a focus during your meditation exercises.

Bloom Bright

You bloom wherever you are planted. For example, you may have an idea or expectation in your mind that before you can bloom you have to be in a certain phase of your life, have a particular situation, or have more money. This is a belief, not a truth. Allow your happiness to bloom wherever and whenever you can by reminding yourself always that *I am blooming*.

You can blossom in any area of your life. Whether you are a mother with small children, exploring a new hobby that brings you joy, or are in the middle of your career blooming, you are thriving and growing through your relationship with energy. By simply choosing to breathe into this moment, you are blooming.

Happiness is the consequence of personal effort. You fight for it, strive for it, insist upon it, and sometimes even travel around the world looking for it. You have to participate relentlessly in the manifestations of your own blessings. And once you have achieved a state of happiness, you must never become lax about maintaining it. You must make a mighty effort to keep swimming upward into that happiness forever, to stay afloat on top of it.

—ELIZABETH GILBERT
American author

See Yourself Reaching Your Goal

What's your primary personal goal? Is it to lose weight, spend less, or earn more money? Whatever it is, write out an affirmation for achieving it. For example: *From now on at mealtimes, I will eat one-third less* or *I will walk for a half hour each day.* Try to keep your affirmation succinct and to the point. That way, it will be easy to recall and repeat at least three times during the day. The more specific your affirmation, the more effective it will be in helping you attain your goal.

Fulfill a Dream

When you put your dreams on hold to help someone else attain his or hers, your selfless action is praiseworthy. However, if you wait too long to chase your own visions, conditions for achieving them may change, your priorities might shift, or you may abandon all hope of ever attaining your dreams. You get married, have children, and realize that you are too busy meeting the demands of daily life head-on. Alternatively, perhaps you still secretly nurture the idea of achieving your cherished dream and just thinking about it fills you with excitement, energy, and a sense of adventure.

A ritual might help jump-start it again. Begin this process by writing your dream on a card in felt-tip marker. Holding the card in your palms, do the following:

1. Mentally banish fear; release limited and discouraging beliefs.
2. Kindle feelings of self-worth for your desire to have that dream.
3. Ask the universe for what you want; use precise language.
4. Open yourself to opportunities that make achieving your dream possible.
5. Let go and trust that your dream has moved from a state of improbable to certain attainment.

Use Your Skills

Fear of being judged can hold you back from putting your skills and assets out there for the world to see. Be proud of the skills, knowledge, and experience you have, and put them to good use going after the things that will make you happy. Don't hesitate to toot your own horn! Gain the confidence to do so by saying this mantra: *Now that I have released excess fear of being judged, I choose to respect my talents and strengths.* If you have been working behind the scenes, supporting the success of others, perhaps it is time to make a shift and allow yourself to manifest some of the creative talents and insights you have gathered. Begin the process with this mantra.

✦

Success is getting what you want, happiness is wanting what you get.

—W.P. KINSELLA
Canadian author

Be Happier at Work

Think of three things you could do to make yourself happier on the job. Would listening to your favorite music lift your spirits? How about seeing pictures of your family members taped to the bottom of your computer screen—would that inspire you to be happy? Or would checking your email at noon instead of when you first arrive at work keep your mood elevated throughout the morning? Find ways to be happy while at work, and your creativity and productivity are likely to rise along with your mood.

Convince Yourself to Be Positive

Perhaps you are nervous about an upcoming situation, and your mind keeps going over all the things that could go wrong. Instead of letting a barrage of negative thoughts take over your life, create a list of positive affirmations to counter the negativity. Suppose you are nervous about going to a party where you will know no one except the hostess, who will obviously be very busy. Repeating a positive phrase like *I will be relaxed, sociable, and have a really fun time* fifty times a day every day before the party (in five sets of ten) will create an expectation in your mind that your brain will be happy to fulfill.

Manifest Wealth

Monetary wealth might not bring true happiness, but it sure helps with a lot of the small nuisances in life. Don't be afraid to search out and try to manifest this material wealth by saying (either out loud or silently to yourself): *I am wealthy.*

As you use this mantra, notice what feelings and emotions surface. Sometimes people shy away from pursuing or exhibiting wealth because they learned to associate the rich with greed, stinginess, and ignorance. The negative stereotypes abound: flashy living, insensitive behavior, unbridled consumption. These are beliefs, not truths. Not all wealthy people are inconsiderate or detached from others. This may be a tough pill to swallow. Breathe as you engage with the mantra, release the feelings that show up, and see being wealthy as no different than being worry-free. Having wealth can be very empowering, as it gives you the freedom to support others in many ways.

✦

It's been my experience that you can nearly always enjoy things if you make up your mind firmly that you will.

—L.M. MONTGOMERY
Canadian author

Stop Negative Thoughts

Some of us can get so good at negative or obsessive thinking that we do it without even being consciously aware that we're doing it. You may think *I know I'll make a poor impression at this job interview!* the second you set up the interview. This type of negative thinking can happen faster than you can manufacture happy thoughts to counter it. The good news is that you can learn to interrupt these negative thoughts and then deal more realistically with them. One tactic is to interrupt negative thoughts by simply saying *Stop!* to yourself. Then switch to a positive thought before any other troubling thoughts emerge. A new, more optimistic thought—such as *I will be relaxed, positive, and learn a lot from my interview!*—will allow you to stop your negative thinking. This is a simple but highly effective technique.

Replace Negative Self-Talk

The greatest obstacle to achieving what we want and finding happiness is ourselves. Time and again we talk ourselves out of being happy, sending negative vibrations throughout the universe. This is an exercise to do if you find that your affirmations are not working and something seems to be blocking your ability to attract what you want.

1. Sit quietly and clear your mind, concentrating on your breathing.
2. When your mind is calm and unburdened, review your thoughts during the past twenty-four hours.
3. How many of these thoughts were positive and affirming?
4. How many of these thoughts were negative self-talk or not accurate portrayals of reality?
5. If the negative thoughts have been outweighing the positive ones, flip the equation. Strengthen your positive thoughts, making them as specific as possible.

Love Yourself

You cannot be happy if you are not happy with who you are. Bring happiness to yourself by repeating the mantra, *I love being me.* Being you means you are able to allow your own thoughts, feelings, and beliefs to emerge with honor and respect. This does not mean you have to act on every little thing. Notice if you start to compare yourself to others or question your abilities and strengths. Take these doubts as a sign that you may be veering from your sense of being. Your path is always being shaped by the way you respond to what is happening inside of you. To get back on your course, put your attention on the now and recite this mantra.

◆

Attitude is a choice.
Happiness is a
choice. Optimism
is a choice.
Kindness is a choice.
Giving is a choice.
Respect is a choice.
Whatever choice you
make makes you.
Choose wisely.

—ROY T. BENNETT
Author

Remember That Happiness
Is a Journey

If you look back over the past week and remember moments of happiness (even if they're only fleeting) but find that your memories are dominated by moments of stress, anxiety, frustration, exasperation, sadness, resentment, jealousy, impatience, worry, concern, or anger, grab a cup of your favorite tea, put your feet up, and consider this: happy isn't something you feel only after you've accomplished everything you want to achieve in life. Nope. It's available to you during every step of the journey...but you make the choice of whether or not you experience that happiness.

Practice Deep Breathing

If you aren't living your best life now, what's holding you back? An honest exploration of that question can help you decide how to make yourself happier. Many tools are available today to transform the life you have into the one you want. Remember that your life's journey is what matters, not the destination. How will you breathe forth an inspired life and manifest your great gifts—qualities, virtues, talents, and abilities—in the world? Begin by deep breathing. Sit with a straight spine, palms open on your thighs. Inhale to the count of four and exhale to the count of eight. On each inhalation, ask yourself: *What do I love doing so much that it makes my spirit lighter, my heart happier, and my whole being feel rapture at the thought of doing it?* Exhale and sit in silence as the answer comes.

Tell Yourself: Fear Is Not Real

Here's the thing: fear is not real. Yup, that's right, fear is not real. When you are experiencing symptoms of fear it sure feels real, though, doesn't it? The way you see the world is affected when you are in fear and your energy is not circulating properly. Rather than seeing choices, you see limitations; rather than seeing love and happiness, you see hurt and resentment.

Take a few moments now to connect with your breath. Tell yourself, *Fear is an illusion. Love is the only thing that is real.* On the inhale, inflate your lower abdomen and take in one slow, rhythmic breath. Allow the energy of fear to transform into courage, strength, and (with practice) love. State this mantra three to five times and then take one full complete breath (inhale to the count of three and exhale to the count of three). Imagine these words as energy moving freely through your body.

✦

The best way to cheer yourself is to try to cheer somebody else up.

—MARK TWAIN
American author

Bake Cookies for the Office Grouch

If someone in your office often scowls, chronically complains, or flies into fits with little or no provocation, offer him or her a plate of warm cookies. Even if your cookies are refused, you can be assured that you at least tried to bring a little pleasure into that person's life. This gesture may work...or it may not. Some people get so used to being unhappy and feeling like the whole world is against them that they are outside of their comfort zone when someone does do something unexpected and nice for them. The truth is that the grouch is probably hungry for friendship and attention and ending their negativity can bring a lot more happiness into *your* life too.

Shower Those Who Love You with Appreciation

Don't miss the opportunity to express a thank you to people you love and who love and support you—your family. If you feel appreciation when someone clears the dinner table, takes out the trash, or puts a load of towels in the washer—thereby easing your workload that might already demand you take a thousand steps a day—tell that person how much you are grateful for his or her efforts.

When you assume that your gratitude is understood and no words are needed, you are robbing that person of a gift that could mean the world to him or her. Offer him a hug. Tell her with genuine sincerity how important she is in your life. Show love and appreciation at every opportunity.

Even when others aren't around, you can reinforce your attitude of gratitude. Pluck a leaf of rose geranium and hold it beneath your nose. Breathe in the calm as you close your eyes and say a prayer thanking the universe for those who love and support you and whom you cherish. Set off on a walk. Mentally call forth each person whom you love and tell every one: *Thank you for being in my life*. Feel grateful that they are walking through the journey of life with you.

Help Your Community

Public health researchers have found that people who volunteer get multiple health benefits from the experience, including less depression, greater feelings of well-being, and a 22 percent lower risk of dying. Your soul wants to contribute to something greater than you. As a human being, you can have all the money and fame in the world; however, if you do not feel like you are contributing to the world in some way, you will feel unsatisfied. Taking time to contribute to your surroundings can change all of this. Whether it's taking a moment to pick up a piece of trash, donating a few items, or volunteering at a local charity, contributing to your community not only helps other people but also makes you happier. After you complete a day of giving back, reaffirm the happiness you experienced in helping others by saying, *I am a contributor to my community.*

✦

The happiness
of your life depends
upon the quality of
your thoughts.

—MARCUS AURELIUS
Roman emperor and author of Meditations

Reminisce

The happiness that can come from reminiscing about happy memories is as real as the feelings that happened during the actual event. In fact, people who frequently reminisce about positive life events are the most likely to be happy. So take photos, make scrapbooks, bring home souvenirs, call an old friend, watch your favorite movies…do whatever you need to do to relive those positive memories.

Develop Deep Self-Love

During infancy and early childhood, a person must receive love and emotional connections if he or she is to feel worthy and lovable as an adult. When those basic needs aren't met, the adult struggles with relationship and abandonment issues. However, no matter what your childhood was like, it's never too late to tap into the universe's infinite reservoir of love, and use that to create a happier and healthier you. See your body, mind, and spirit as unique and worthy of self-love. Loving yourself, you are then able to share your love and happiness with others. This self-care isn't narcissism but rather a cultivation of a tender loving-kindness to achieve healthy selfhood.

Begin writing daily in a journal or a Smash book (part journal, part scrapbook) that celebrates your life. In it, write a daily positive affirmation to yourself. Keep expressions simple; for example, *My body is healthy* or *My heart is peaceful and loving* or *My mind is imaginative.* Or, *I am happy.* Paste or draw images and symbols from your meditation and dreams. Jot down any inner guidance. See your mind as wildly creative; see your body as an old friend that has brought you from infancy to adulthood, ever loyal and faithful and never abandoning you.

Expand Your Awareness

It can be so easy to get caught up in other people's descriptions of happiness. A *Facebook* post, bit of celebrity news, or Snapchat photo compels you to live someone else's moment (even if it's fixed or filtered or edited), and it can give you a false impression of what true happiness is. When you focus too much on other people as a measure of your own happiness, you inevitably disconnect from your source of happiness—yourself.

Happiness is an internal state of being, not an external place you have to find. Recite *As I expand my awareness, energy flows freely through me* to redirect and expand your awareness to your internal source of happiness.

✦

Man only likes to count his troubles; he doesn't calculate his happiness.

—FYODOR DOSTOYEVSKY
Russian author

Stop Complaining

Seeing as the brain has a tendency to focus on the negative, complaining may in fact be a natural human reaction. Still, that doesn't mean complaining is the best reaction. Dwelling on the worst of the world is not good for your body or your mood. Besides, when has complaining ever gotten you anywhere? All it does is reinforce negativity. So rather than complaining about something, try to focus on something else, something positive. You'll be happier.

Write a Check to Yourself

Writing an abundance check to yourself might take only a minute or two of your time, but it could pay off substantially in a newfound prosperity. Consider how it's worked for others such as the actor Jim Carrey who—as the story goes—wrote himself a check for $10 million that he carried around before he became a household name. Do the new moon check ritual once a month.

1. On a blank check (a real one or one you create to look real), write today's date.
2. Make it out to your full legal name.
3. Leave blank the dollar amount box and line but on the signature line, write: *Law of Abundance*.
4. Write in the memo sector: *Paid in full*.
5. Take out the check at the beginning of each new moon and hold the paper in your palms while you visualize the dollar amount you desire to attract that month.
6. Feel happiness when you are inspired with ideas for opportunities for making money as well as when money flows in; don't forget to express gratitude (write thank-you notes and tuck them into a box where you keep the check).

Look at Your Strengths

Research has shown that focusing on your strengths decreases depression and increases healthy behaviors such as an active lifestyle. You can acknowledge and affirm your strengths by telling yourself, *I believe in my abilities and strengths.*

In order to focus on your strengths, you must first recognize what they are. Ask yourself two questions:

1. In what areas do I feel strong?
2. In what areas am I getting stronger?

These areas can be as simple as feeling strong in a particular skill such as cooking, drawing, or reading. You may have strong interpersonal skills, or maybe you are pretty good at getting organized or using a computer. Take a moment now to acknowledge what you are good at as well as the skills you look forward to developing.

◆

Today is a new day!

Many will seize
this day.

Many will live it
to the fullest.

Why not you?

—STEVE MARABOLI
American motivational speaker and author

Spearhead a Pet Project

If there's a project that you're itching to take on, then make it happen. Not only will you gain a sense of satisfaction from a job well done, you'll also impress the higher-ups at work. Start with a discussion with a trusted colleague or supervisor who is empowered with the knowledge necessary to limit or expand the scope of the project and who knows what is needed to get a go-ahead. Then dig deep, do the work, write a project proposal, and volunteer to oversee it from start to finish. Your passion will be the driving force to manifest the project and your creativity and drive will ensure that your managers and bosses take notice. A self-starter with a can-do attitude is an asset to any company. Although the satisfaction of hard work well done is its own reward, most people find great happiness from external validation of their efforts.

Greet the Dawn

Scientific studies have found that early risers are healthier, happier, and more productive than their night owl counterparts. Waking up early doesn't mean you must leap out of bed. Before throwing off those covers to drink water, attend to hygiene, exercise, and eat breakfast, take some time to linger in that quiet space between sleeping and wakefulness with a morning ritual that focuses on gathering in positive energy. This space holds for you gifts of extraordinary phenomena, including:

- Intense imagery
- Audible sounds of nature, voices, and music
- Taste sensations
- Touch sensitivity
- Otherworldly scents of incense or florals or unidentifiable smells
- A heightened sense of presence

Since ancient times, yogis have hailed the hour and a half before sunrise as the most auspicious time of the day. Some believe that accessing the positivity and power of deeper meditative states is easier in the predawn when your mind is still. Keep a small stone by your bedside. Hold it on awakening to remind you to generate positive vibes from this time and take them with you into your day.

Cultivate Opportunities

If you are concerned that your opportunities are limited—perhaps you have a belief that there are only so many jobs, or that all the good jobs are taken—then tell yourself, *Opportunities come my way easily.* Be mindful that if you tie up your time and energy with something you don't like, or a job that may be draining you, that choice could interfere with your happiness and your opportunity to create something new. Recite this mantra daily and avoid making choices that don't lead to your true bliss because you fear you will never have another chance. Opportunities are always available. Allow this mantra to increase your ability to trust this.

◆

It was only a
sunny smile, and
little it cost in the
giving, but like
morning light it
scattered the night
and made the day
worth living.

—F. SCOTT FITZGERALD
American author

Smile at Yourself

It may sound silly, but smiling causes an emotional response in your body that can actually make you feel happier. Smiling at other people can make them and you feel happier, but smiling at yourself in the mirror can have the added effect of boosting your self-esteem and self-love. Imagine smiling at yourself in the mirror every morning—think about what that would do for your confidence and mood throughout the day!

Use the Language of Gratitude

If you've forgotten the language of gratitude, you'll never be on speaking terms with happiness, according to an old adage. As it turns out, expressing gratitude has measurable benefits—among them, increased happiness, less depression, and a heightened sense of well-being that is noticeable by others. Dr. Robert A. Emmons, a world-renowned expert on gratitude, has said that grateful people develop a particular linguistic style that includes words such as *givers*, *gifts*, *blessings*, *blessed*, *fortune*, *fortunate*, and *abundance*. So it might be wise to not only count your blessings but also tell others about them in language that reflects their specialness. While you're at it, let your gratitude shine through sincere and appreciative language delivered with a gracious smile or a warm hug. The following meditation can help you develop an attitude of gratitude:

1. Do some quiet breathing to still the mind.
2. Center your awareness in your heart.
3. Think of blessings you already have and feel grateful for them.
4. Start a mental conversation about three specific things with which you feel blessed.
5. Explain in detail why those three are special. Use words like those listed by Dr. Emmons.
6. Reflect on how you are loved and valued and your life has been enriched.
7. Feel contented and happy. End your prayer with an appreciative thank you for all your blessings, especially those three.

Beautiful Inside and Out

Beauty is much more than skin deep. Someone may be attractive on the outside, yet be riddled with insecurity, hatred, and jealousy on the inside. This can make him or her challenging to be around, and it may be difficult to maintain a relationship with this person. True beauty happens when it is illuminated through you—when your happiness, love, and contentment shine through your speech and actions. Keep this in mind by repeating *Beautiful inside and out* to yourself.

According to the website *WebMD*, being stressed all the time can actually deprive you of vital nutrients necessary for sustaining physical health. Stress can negatively affect the vitality of your skin and hair, and can even cause high blood pressure, headaches, and stomachaches. Incorporating mantras into your life is one way to de-stress and ensure true beauty.

I do not miss childhood, but I miss the way I took pleasure in small things, even as greater things crumbled. I could not control the world I was in, could not walk away from things or people or moments that hurt, but I found joy in the things that made me happy.

—NEIL GAIMAN
English author

Snuggle with Something

If you are like many people, as a child you had a little pillow or a security blanket that got you through the night. As an adult facing a crisis, you may wish you had something tangible like that to give you comfort. If you don't have a favorite blanket or pillow, look in the linen closet and see if there's a comfy throw, a worn afghan, or a silky coverlet you could use. Or go to the clearance table at your local department store and pick out something that could become a new favorite security blanket. As a child, you loved your blankey because it was yours and only yours. It had your scent on it. You knew what it felt like and looked like even with your eyes closed. The next time life is not going your way, seek comfort in what's familiar and what makes you feel safe—wrap yourself in your blanket and let your inner child feel safe and comforted.

Invite Your Inner Child to Play

Sometimes you just have to let your hair down and have some fun if you're stuck in a rut and can't figure out how to bust out. We were all happy children once. Somewhere deep inside you is the inner child you long ago forgot about. Invite him or her out to play.

Do what used to make you happy. Was it painting, kicking a soccer ball around, or dancing in front of the sliding glass door where you could see your image? Perhaps you were the kind of child who loved playing with Play-Doh, calculating hopscotch squares, jumping rope, playing a musical instrument, or drawing for hours under a tree. Find that wild child again.

Afraid someone might see you? Forget about that. Find an old Hula-Hoop. Put it around your waist and start swerving in circles. Stretch out your arms. Whirl and twirl. Close your eyes. Peek out every now and again to avoid colliding with a bush or tree. Enjoy the movement. Feel young. Feel renewed. It's exhilarating.

Live Well

To be well, you have to live well. Tell yourself that you are doing just that by saying the *I live well* mantra and bring happiness into your life. Rather than focusing on what you can't do, or your limitations, this mantra reminds you that you are both the author and the illustrator of your life. Before repeating the mantra, ask yourself what living well looks like for you. How does it feel? What would you imagine yourself doing if you were living well? Repeat this mantra several times and allow yourself to visualize what this would look, feel, and sound like.

True happiness is to enjoy the present, without anxious dependence upon the future, not to amuse ourselves with either hopes or fears but to rest satisfied with what we have, which is sufficient, for he that is so wants nothing. The greatest blessings of mankind are within us and within our reach. A wise man is content with his lot, whatever it may be, without wishing for what he has not.

—SENECA
Roman philosopher

The best years of your life are the ones in which you decide your problems are your own. You do not blame them on your mother, the ecology, or the president. You realize that you control your own destiny.

—ALBERT ELLIS
American psychologist

Dance Around the Kitchen

Start your day with a little salsa, mambo, cha-cha, or your favorite dance steps as you make your way over to measure the coffee, add the water, and turn on the pot. Dance until the coffee is ready. Have a cup and then dance some more! Start your fancy footwork in your kitchen and jig throughout your house. If you have to leave for work, dance your way to your dressing room and keep moving while you do your makeup. Dance over to pick up your purse, briefcase, and car keys…and then dance right into the garage. Keep moving and feel your smiles emerge and pounds melt away.

Plant Yourself in the Moment

Grounding yourself into the present moment is an essential part of being truly happy. When you're feeling stressed or out of focus, picture in your mind a large, old tree and repeat this mantra: *Being firmly grounded into my body offers me peace.* See the tree's strong root system and flexible branches. Picture its peacefulness and the nourishment it brings to its environment.

You are no different than this tree. You also have a strong root system, capable of providing security and peace. When using this mantra, soften your solar plexus (navel area) and when you exhale, imagine directing your energy out through your legs into the ground. Allow this mantra to support your energy by grounding it into the earth through this tree visualization.

Be Aware

A simple shift in perception can move you closer to happiness. All you have to do is become aware of yourself in this moment. Help yourself become more aware by repeating the mantra, *My awareness is enough.*

Awareness means consciousness. To be aware is to notice and be awake to your surroundings. If you are distracted or consumed by thinking, your awareness may be low. Choose to increase it by taking a moment to pause and listen to your breath. As you repeat this mantra, listen and feel your breath moving in and out of your body. Your breath will anchor you to the present moment. Being aware and fully present makes it easier to recognize happiness when and where it's available.

✦

Those who are
not looking for
happiness are the
most likely to find it,
because those who
are searching forget
that the surest way
to be happy is to seek
happiness for others.

—REVEREND MARTIN LUTHER KING JR.
American civil rights leader

Give Ten Minutes of Undivided Attention to Each Family Member

Some days it seems that everybody is clamoring for your attention. But when it comes to family members, it's important that you give it to them. Ten minutes often is not enough to really get started talking, but it shows your loved ones that you care deeply about what troubles them and that you want to help. Even if your help is just listening to them vent, do it. You can always set aside another ten minutes to continue the discussion at a later time. Consider the alternative. Brushing them aside for more urgent matters sends the wrong signal. Make time for loved ones before they leave your nest. Isn't it true that you are happiest when you know that they are happy too?

Celebrate Your Friendships

Friends bring out the best in you; they act as your reflecting mirrors, revealing your wholesomeness and best features as well as untoward, unwholesome, or unseemly actions, which they discourage. If you have a vision but can't achieve it alone, you surround yourself with the team that can make your vision a reality. It's a concept that works well in business and also in friendships.

Some life experiences are difficult and challenging to face without support—for example, a natural catastrophe, life-threatening illness, business setback, or career or personal loss. Pals who care as much about you as you respect and cherish them will accompany you on your life's journey and help you navigate the pitfalls and obstacles even as they lift and inspire you. They're loyal and will keep your confidences. They rejoice at your successes and good fortune. Waft around some rose essential oil and light a pink candle (pink and rose are colors associated with love and compassion) and then write personal notes to your closest friends, expressing heartfelt appreciation for the gifts they bring to your life.

Share the Good

Have you ever had a positive or kind thought and held yourself back from sharing it? Perhaps you loved a yoga class but never took the time to express it to the teacher, or you were touched by the kind gesture of another but felt awkward letting them know.

Remind yourself to spread joy by telling yourself, *I have something good to say and I choose to say it!* Giving other people compliments or thanking them for their time and attention brings happiness to both parties. Let's face it, even the most confident people could use a pat on the back now and then. Make a point to let others know they are doing a good job and watch how your happiness increases too!

✦

I think happiness
is what makes
you pretty. Period.
Happy people are
beautiful. They
become like a mirror
and they reflect
that happiness.

—DREW BARRYMORE
American actress

Let Go of Negative Body Images

There is no one "correct" body type. Sure, you should strive to be as healthy as you can, but if you feel comfortable in your own skin and you're happy with your life, other people's opinions of body types shouldn't matter. Don't let other people tell you you're not beautiful or that you could be more beautiful if you only did this or that. Your opinion of your body is the only one that matters. If you are not happy in your own skin, then take steps to improve yourself, but only if you truly desire to make those changes.

Nourish Your Skin

You feel more empowered when you look and feel great. Your outer appearance reflects the inner you. The condition of your skin is closely related to your overall well-being. Follow these basics to keep yourself at your best, inside and out:

- Meditate to feel peace and happiness.
- Deep breathe to bring more oxygen to your cells.
- Get enough sleep.
- Eat nutritious foods.
- Drink lots of water.
- Limit your skin's exposure to the sun, environmental pollution, and toxic substances.
- Find and use a nourishing all-natural face cream or make your own with rich emollients such as almond oil, vitamin E oil, coconut oil, beeswax, and shea butter. A few drops of essential oil for fragrance are optional.
- If you want luminous beauty that glows throughout your lifetime, look inside yourself. Frequent contact with your inner luminosity will manifest externally, in joy, serenity, and grace.
- Bust stress by eliminating stressors where possible; sink deeply into moments of tranquility.

Let Love Make You Young

Love literally turns the clock back on aging. It does this by raising your endorphin levels while decreasing the production of stress hormones such as cortisol, causing waves of joy and happiness to stream into you. Celebrate this happiness by reminding yourself that *I am bursting with vitality and youth*.

Love is one of your highest vibrational emotions. The movement of your loving energy cleanses and nourishes your body, skin, mind, and internal organs. Focus on love daily, and you'll activate the genes responsible for supporting your life with grace and ease.

◆

Happiness is
not a goal...it's a
by-product of a
life well lived.

—ELEANOR ROOSEVELT
Thirty-second first lady of the United States

Attract the People You Want in Your Life

If you are seeking loyalty and trust in your friendships or in a romantic relationship, first cultivate those qualities within yourself and then demonstrate them to others—in doing so, you become a magnet for exactly what you want. Similarly, if you seek a gentle, loving person as a life partner, avoid someone with a mercurial, volatile, or temperamental nature. Although opposites do sometimes attract, you'll most likely be happiest with a kindred spirit.

Cultivate Your Uniqueness

Your values, beliefs, feelings, and opinions—what you bring out into the world of your inner being rather than what the world brings you—partly define you. You can let go of a professional or personal self-image that depends on the affiliations and groups you belong to or labels others put on you. Become more aware of your inner magnificence by doing the following:

- Be courageous and confident.
- Express your uniqueness through creative ideas.
- Listen to the voice of your soul (intuition).
- Speak your truth.
- Love your journey more than any destination along the way.

Use a diffuser with rosemary-scented oil to permeate an area where you can sit and detect the odor. As your brain brightens with clarity and energy, meditate on your unique inner attributes, talents, traits, wisdom, and gifts of the spirit and how you might use them for your own happiness and that of others.

Be Who You Are

One of the simplest and most profound mantras is *So Hum*—
"I am that I am." Meditating on this simple phrase, you penetrate
your layers of protection and self-criticism and come to the core
of your happiness. As you repeat *So Hum* over and over, you
bring your awareness to who you are at the core—the quiet, still
place. You discover simply that you exist, that you are.

✦

The more you
praise and
celebrate your life,
the more there is in
life to celebrate.

—OPRAH WINFREY
American entrepreneur, philanthropist, and TV host

Pat Your Own Back

You praise your friends, your coworkers, and your spouse whenever they accomplish something praiseworthy, so why not give yourself some praise? You're not being a braggart or egotistical when you acknowledge that you finished a task or made a breakthrough—you work very hard and accomplish many things that no one but you ever recognizes. If you finally played a complicated piano composition all the way through or found an ingenious way to increase your project's budget, tell yourself how wonderfully brilliant and accomplished you are. Bask in the glory of the moment! You deserve it.

Note the Value in Your Life

Noticing the ways your life imparts value to others and brings happiness to you helps you see all of the good things in your life. When you work to clear away old mental tapes and emotional baggage, you make it possible for energy that's been impeded or stuck to shift. Positive thinking, energetic and enthusiastic action, and a sense of personal worth bring empowerment.

When you want true happiness, the secret is to give first and then hold up your basket to the universe to receive. Purchase or make a receptacle such as a brass pot, a crystal bowl, a lovely basket, or a decorative box to hold treasures that show up in your life. Devise a ritual that magnetizes this container with abundance-attracting energy. For example, dip your finger into running water and run it around the rim or opening of your receptacle. Hold the bowl, basket, or box up and ask for blessings to surround, permeate, and fill the bowl.

Expect the Best

Since energy cannot be destroyed, neither can your dreams. If you desire a life of abundance—whether it be in health, happiness, or finances—it is yours. If you ever feel low, like good things aren't coming your way, remind yourself that *I deserve everything I desire.* Keep striving for your happiness and eventually it will come. Know that you are already worthy and enough.

✦

My happiness is
not the means
to any end. It is the
end. It is its own goal.
It is its own purpose.

—AYN RAND
Russian-American philosopher and author

Do Something Fun

This may seem simplistic, but many, many people go through their days without doing anything fun. Studies have clearly shown that engaged activity breaks obsessive thoughts. Doing something fun will get you off the beaten track so that you can put things into perspective and get rid of negative feelings or thoughts that have been weighing you down. Not to mention the obvious: it's fun! So whether your fun is skydiving, reading a great novel, swimming, playing with kids, or having a little romantic encounter with your significant other, the lesson here is to stop wishing or thinking about it—get out there and do it.

Wish Happiness

Wishing happiness for all beings can take practice. There's a special kind of meditation that is used for cultivating this ability. It's called *metta meditation*. There are variations, but in general this is how you practice metta:

1. Sit in a comfortable, seated position for meditation.
2. Close your eyes, and follow your breath as it goes in and out several times.
3. Say this to yourself: *May I be happy. May I be healthy. May I know peace.*
4. Bring to mind someone you love dearly. Hold this person in your mind's eye. Repeat the same wish: *May you be happy. May you be healthy. May you know peace.*
5. Bring to mind someone who is an acquaintance whom you have good feelings toward, and don't know very well. Perhaps it's someone who works in the same building as you, or the person at the post office who always helps you mail your packages. Hold this person in your mind's eye, and say: *May you be happy. May you be healthy. May you know peace.*
6. Now repeat this for all beings: *May all beings be happy. May all beings be healthy. May all beings know peace.* When you are finished, open your eyes.

Follow Your Heart

Many people have been told to do one thing, but their hearts steered them to another. If something feels right in your heart, it probably is right for you. In your mind you may doubt your choices or abilities, but your heart usually gently tugs you back to what feels right. When you're conflicted about a decision, tell yourself, *My heart leads me right now; I listen to what feels right.* Go with this. Listen. Trust that your heart knows the way to happiness. Your heart is highly intelligent. The more you listen, the stronger your ability to do what feels right will come through.

All I ask is one thing, and I'm asking this particularly of young people: please don't be cynical. I hate cynicism, for the record, it's my least favorite quality and it doesn't lead anywhere. Nobody in life gets exactly what they thought they were going to get. But if you work really hard and you're kind, amazing things will happen.

—CONAN O'BRIEN
American comedian and TV host

Notice the Wonders of Life

Incredible things are happening all around you all the time! Just for a moment, notice the wonders of life: look at the way light shimmers on dew drops clinging to an elaborate spider's web, smell the scent of lilacs after a hard rain, watch the majestic flight of eagles, savor the taste of a freshly cut watermelon, gaze at the pattern of a piece of gum stuck to the pavement, admire the vibrant color of a peacock feather, hear the sizzle of a marshmallow toasted over a crackling fire. Noticing life's little details will fire up your imagination and your natural inquisitiveness about the world.

Savor Something Good

Your brain is wired to scan for and remember adverse events—this "negativity bias" helped humans adapt to threats in their environment. What was great for our evolution is now a root of stress and anxiety. To help re-train your brain, dedicate some time to reveling in good memories.

1. Sit quietly and call up a happy moment.
2. Relive that memory in the greatest detail you can muster, and let the good feelings soak into your cells.
3. Appreciate the positive things you experience even more, which boosts gratitude and contentment.

Honor the Good in Others

The word *namaste*, which you'll often hear at the end of meditation or yoga class, is actually a mantra that means "The light in me sees the light in you." Another translation would be "The good in me sees the honorable and good in you." When you recite this mantra, know that it does not apply exclusively to people. You can state it to a tree, animal, or even an idea. It's a gentle way to bless the world and spread happiness throughout the universe.

✦

We all live with
the objective of
being happy; our
lives are all different
and yet the same.

—ANNE FRANK
German-born Jewish diarist

Stargaze

Looking up at a sky full of stars is not only a meditative exercise that helps you feel more calm and centered, it also teaches you perspective. Contemplating the vastness and distance of space and the universe gives you a new angle on your life and problems…and stargazing helps you discover the beauty of nature too. Stargazing can also be a kind of meditation; the calm peacefulness of gazing up at the stars helps quiet your mind and the stresses of your day. As an additional bonus the time spent outside, even as little as twenty minutes, will also be a big happiness booster.

Clarify Your Intention

You've always wanted to go to Peru, see the Andes, the Amazon rainforest, and Machu Picchu. Peruvian landscapes, colonial cathedrals, and ethnic works of art dot your walls. You can't explain the attraction since you don't know any Peruvians, nor have you had any other exposure to the country. Yet when someone asks you where you'd most like to go on vacation, that country pops right up on your lips.

Write out your intention in a clear statement of purpose and then you are ready to break your purpose into smaller, incremental goals. Write down your goals, including a reward for reaching each one. Follow this plan with the following affirmation: *I intend to visit Machu Picchu in May next year.* Stay focused. Do not doubt and you'll get there, because every intention must be answered.

Here's a twice-daily ritual to strengthen your specific intention, whatever it may be. Light a joss stick (of dried perfume paste) or incense to sanctify the space.

1. Sit in your favorite meditation posture with eyes closed and declare your specific intention.
2. Feel worthy. Trust that you've been heard.
3. Visualize your desire manifesting and feel the emotional high.
4. Seize opportunity when it comes; give thanks.

Think Globally

Happiness in your life doesn't have to be limited to only you, your loved ones, or your community. Remember, you are part of a large global community as well and their happiness can affect yours. Remember your global community with the mantra, *May all beings everywhere be happy and free, and may the thoughts, words, and actions of my own life contribute in some way to that happiness and to that freedom for all.*

This mantra reminds us that no one is really free from suffering entirely until we are all free. This is a beautiful chant to teach children or to utilize yourself as a means for increasing happiness worldwide. In light of some of the terror we and our children have been exposed to, whether it's through media or an actual incident, this chant gives us a tangible tool for moving through the overwhelming feelings these images and experiences bring. Remember, fear cannot survive in love. They cannot both exist.

✦

Let the dead
bury the dead,
but while I'm alive,
I must live
and be happy.

—LEO TOLSTOY
Russian author

Flirt with Someone

Flirting is fun and harmless and can make you feel good about yourself. Next time you're in a bookshop or coffee shop—or even a supermarket!—try a little flirting. Let's say you see a great-looking guy thumbing through a travel guide. Or maybe an attractive woman is standing in front of the science fiction novels or shelves of business books. The point is that you like what you see. You could walk over, excuse yourself, and reach past her to retrieve a book that's right in front of her. If you're a bit timid, simply flash a nice smile after making eye contact. Or comment on the travel book he's reading. Is it a guide to Ireland, where you once bicycled through rolling hills? Have you read *Finnegans Wake*? Show your curiosity and interest in the topic (and the person) and get your best flirt on.

Surround Yourself with Meaningful Things

Whether your sanctuary is your home or your office, determine what makes you happy and then choose furniture, art, wall colors, books, and pictures of people who inspire you. Perhaps it's a settee you found in a vintage shop that lifts your spirits. Or your grandmother's drop-leaf claw-foot table that she left you in her will with a note taped to it explaining she knew how much you always loved it. Items with meaning should find a place in the interiors where you live and work precisely because they hold special memories and significance for you. Like everything in the universe, those well-loved pieces are permeated with subtle joyful energy from the people who've loved you and also used and loved those pieces.

Think of a beloved relative who has passed away to whom you'd like to pay tribute. Perhaps you have an old framed photo. If not, find one you like and frame it. Light a white sage smudge stick to clear the energy in the area where the picture will hang. Admire the picture when it's hung. Offer words of welcome and ask that ancestor to bless you and your space.

Tell Yourself It Will All Work Out

Mantras don't always have to be entirely true to help you find happiness. Sometimes little white lies are needed to bring yourself joy and help you remember the good times. For example, telling yourself *Things always work out for me* can bring you peace and happiness even if it's not always entirely true.

You will find that there are many times in your life when this mantra can give you the strength to believe in something, even if there is no proof. Perhaps you are waiting to hear about a job offer, hoping to get into a particular college, or maybe you are supporting a loved one through a rough situation. Choose to believe everything will (and has always) worked out for you and everyone else. See yourself as resilient and strong. Remember, saying something as if it is true and happening is very powerful.

✦

It's a helluva start, being able to recognize what makes you happy.

—LUCILLE BALL
American actress and comedian

Plan Your Dream Vacation

The anticipation of an event can often bring just as much happiness as the actual event, so start planning the vacation of your dreams now! Even if you don't currently have the funds to take the trip, start looking into the details. You'll notice your spirits start to lift.

Maybe you've always wanted to go trekking in the Himalayas or visit a rainforest. No matter your ideal destination, start researching the various aspects of your trip and formulate a plan on how to make your dream a reality.

Find Your Dream Job

There's nothing worse than having to play mind games to get up and go to work each day at a job you hate. If you find yourself in that situation, don't waste a minute more living your life in that mode. You could stay in that line of work, but it's pretty much a guarantee that you're not going to be happy.

If you don't know what line of work you'd be good at, consider types of activities that make you happy when you're doing them. Don't be timid. Go for what speaks to your passion. Formulate a clear intention of the kind of job you want to manifest. Find some tangible object such as a car key if you want to design cars or work at an auto dealership, an egg cup if you want to be a farmer and raise chickens, or a packaged toothbrush if you want to work in a dentist's office. If you have loftier intentions, that's terrific. Just find an object that represents your dream job. Morning, noon, and night, hold that object in your hand and recite your intention. Feel it, believe it, visualize it, affirm it, and give thanks for it until the job shows up.

Live Passionately

Anyone can meander through life, going with the flow and not feeling much of anything. However, those people are almost always unhappy. Be passionate and proclaim to the world, *Passion, I am that!*

Passion gives you the ability to see the world in color. When you are focused on comparing and contrasting, you are in black-or-white (all-or-none) thinking. Black-or-white thinking narrows your focus. As this occurs, you may become tied to time and responsibilities. When you view things from passion (color), you are living in the flow (timelessness). Sure, you still get things done, but your life is fueled by your passion rather than your attachment to controlling the course of your day.

◆

I, not events, have the power to make me happy or unhappy today. I can choose which it shall be. Yesterday is dead, tomorrow hasn't arrived yet. I have just one day, today, and I'm going to be happy in it.

—GROUCHO MARX
American actor

Say No

It's easy to say yes—people like you when you say yes to the things they want or need. It's tougher to say no, but sometimes saying no is just the thing you need to feel happier. Is someone trying to push you into doing something you don't have time or the desire to do? Say no. Is someone trying to make you bend on a boundary you feel you need to stand firm on? Say no. Is someone trying to dump a project or task on you? Say no. If you have a hard time saying no, try this: stand in front of a mirror and practice saying, *No, it's not possible*, and then turning and walking away. You never again have to give in when you know you don't want to do something or when you know something is not a good idea. Practice until saying no is as easy as saying yes. Saying no is a powerful tool in your game-of-life chest.

Speak Your Truth

If someone from the past has caused you to doubt the validity of your worth in the world and silenced your voice, find ways to reemerge, gain confidence, and speak out. In the greater universe, we may be tiny specks, but in this world, you are just as important as every other person. To empower your authentic voice, join a book club, community forum, or social group where disseminating ideas and expressing personal opinions are encouraged. Work with a therapist or coach or reflect on your voice by doing the following ritual:

1. Wash a blue lapis lazuli chakra stone in a mild saltwater solution and let it dry in the sun (to absorb solar energy).
2. Lie in the Corpse Pose (a yoga position in which you're flat on your back, palms up at your side) and place the stone over the center of your throat.
3. Meditate on your inner divine nature and that happiness that arises when you use your voice.

Assert Yourself

Having a strong voice not only protects you but builds confidence in yourself. Foster this strong voice by telling yourself, *I choose to speak up and assert myself now*. This mantra encourages you to speak up, ask for help, or let people know if something is bothering you. Break any silence and let go of secrets that you've been hiding. Suppressing your thoughts and feelings can lead to high levels of stress, resentment, and dissatisfaction with the way things are unfolding in your life, preventing you from being truly happy. It can also live in your body like trauma, holding unpleasant memories in place. Use this mantra as a way to strengthen your voice and build courage.

✦

The reason people
find it so hard to be
happy is that they
always see the past
better than it was,
the present worse
than it is, and the
future less resolved
than it will be.

—MARCEL PAGNOL
French filmmaker and playwright

Stop Worrying

We're a society of worriers, but in reality most of the terrible things that we envision happening never do. We're afraid of what might happen (or not happen) with respect to things we can't change (or won't be able to change) and what other people think about us. We worry and we hesitate, and as a consequence, we wind up thinking longer about doing something rather than just doing it. Meanwhile, weeks, months, and years pass, and we are still worried and still unhappy. If you want to be happier, put aside fear and worry and do something! Start something; take a first step. The only thing you should worry about is wasting your days and your life and not doing what you dream about doing.

Make Doing What You Like a Priority

The things you do regularly shape your life much more than the things you do once in a while. So make sure you're regularly doing things that make you happy. What things do you do frequently that make you feel good? It may be cooking a healthy meal, reading a great book, going for a walk, talking to a friend, or something else.

Once a week, make a list of five things that bring you joy. Let this list help you gauge how you're doing—when you notice that you haven't done anything on your list in three days, for example, you know you have to do some re-prioritizing.

Live in the Now

Worrying about the future is an energy drainer. It's a counterproductive means for attempting to control outcome. The more you attempt to control, the more stuck, emotionally fragile, and overwhelmed you may feel. Treat your body as an ally. What is it trying to tell you?

Deferring to your body as a channel of light and love brings you to the present moment, where fear and worry do not exist. Help open this channel wide by repeating the mantra, *I feel the flow of light now*. If you tend to focus on what you have to do or what is left undone, consider reciting this mantra at the beginning and end of each day.

◆

The art of
being happy lies
in the power of
extracting
happiness from
common things.

—HENRY WARD BEECHER
American abolitionist and pastor

Buy Small Things

Instead of buying the latest smartphone, the coolest new car, or the best new laptop, buy several small things: fancy chocolates, a few nice candles, some music for your phone. It will actually make you happier to indulge in frequent small pleasures than to buy more extravagant (and expensive) delights. After all, you don't get twice as much happiness from buying a car that is twice as expensive as another model! Use some of that money to pay for a weekend away with your partner. You'll get far more satisfaction from your getaway weekend than you would from the luxury car.

Fill a Jar with Notes of Thanks

Jars are often filled with good things from a garden—succulent little jams in the smallest containers, relishes and tomato and pumpkin sauces in midsized jars, and juicy peaches and pears, and green beans, corn, and all manner of squash preserved in large ring-top canning jars. Dining on this bounty in the dead of winter helps bring in some of summer's warmth and memories that are sure to bring you joy.

When your garden bounty is through, put your trusty pen to paper and cultivate a bounty of gratitude. Nail a particularly challenging yoga pose and feel over the moon about it? Write it down. When your significant other brings you chocolate and flowers just because, write about how happy he or she made you. After a period of meditation from which you emerge spiritually charged, note how blessed you feel. Write out your gratitude. All these notes get dropped into your garden jar of gratitude.

Make your ritual into three parts: Pay attention to what shows up in your life. Notice how events, people, circumstances, and objects color your emotions, especially when something generates joy, peace, confidence, trust, and appreciation. Take time to write at length about these things through the lens of gratitude and then drop your notes into the jar.

Bask in the Sun's Joy

The sun is one of the greatest sources of happiness and joy on earth. Not only does the sun give you vitamin D, which is essential to maintaining a positive mood and healthy bones, it also strengthens your energy field. Think about how good you feel after sitting (even briefly) in the sun. Give thanks to the sun for your happiness by saying, *Basking in your radiant rays now; thank you, sun, for strengthening my aura.* If you work or live in a high-pressure or negative environment, consider taking time to go outside for a few minutes a day (particularly if it's sunny). Make this mantra a part of your daily routine.

✦

Happiness cannot
be traveled to,
owned, earned,
worn, or consumed.
Happiness is the
spiritual experience
of living every minute
with love, grace,
and gratitude.

—DENIS WAITLEY
American motivational speaker and author

Wear More Color

Studies have shown that color can enhance your mood and make you feel better about yourself. The takeaway? While black may be slimming for your body, it isn't doing much for your mind. Get out of your black clothing rut and add a little color to your wardrobe! You'll notice an improved sense of confidence, and happiness will follow.

Manifest Happiness

The law of attraction is a philosophical idea that asserts that the power of your thought is always drawing to you positive and negative people, objects, situations, and circumstances. Use this power to draw good energy and happiness into your soul. Formulate a clear intention and then infuse it with the belief that you deserve what you ask for; trust that what you ask for, you'll receive; and feelings of confidence, joy, expectancy, and gratitude will follow. Use the following meditation technique to get started:

1. Sit with eyes closed.
2. Visualize a specific object you desire.
3. Mentally state your intention to draw your heart's desire into your life. Be bold and specific in your declaration. For example, if you want a string of beads to use for chanting prayers or a mantra, you might say to yourself: *I desire to manifest a japa mala of 108 sandalwood prayer beads from India tied with red string, and I am drawing it to me now.*
4. Affirm you are deserving and ready to receive. Make a space in your life for the object.
5. Stoke a feeling of jubilation, feeling as you will when the object arrives, not questioning when or how it will come.
6. Feel genuine gratitude and happiness for all that comes to you when you manifest your wants.

Shine Bright

Happy people tend to shine on rather than move on. To move on means to push your feelings down or hold them back, and then go about your way. To shine on means to pause and allow yourself to fully experience what is coming up without judging it. While you pause, quietly repeat *Shine on!* to yourself in order to stay in the right mind-set.

You might feel a twisted feeling in your stomach, tightness in your chest, or clenching of your teeth. Shining on means to trust the inner guidance of your body. Digest your emotions and you will grow (shine) from the experience. Ignore or guard yourself from your emotions and you may find yourself recycling (stuck in) the same emotions and experiences.

◆

Happiness is when what you think, what you say, and what you do are in harmony.

—MAHATMA GANDHI
Indian activist and leader of the Indian Independence Movement

Write a Mission Statement for Your Life

Your mission statement is a blueprint of your vision for your life. When thinking about writing a mission statement, be specific. If you want to have a happy, meaningful life, ask yourself what actions you will need to take and what values and purposes you must have to drive those actions. What is your raison d'être? What is the focus of your life's work? How do the things you do and the way you treat your family and other people reflect your core values? Maybe you prefer to react as life comes at you. But if not, clarify what you want to do with your life. What will give you lasting peace and happiness, when, at the end of your life, you look back at how you lived?

Cultivate Self-Love

Self-love is compassion and caring for the self; it's not "all about me." Self-love is any action that includes behaviors and attitudes that help you better appreciate yourself and your own happiness. Society is always screaming messages that you have to do more, be more, give more. Forget about the accomplishments you haven't achieved yet. Instead, focus on the lovely, unique being that you are. Give attention to what nourishes your spiritual, psychological, and emotional growth. Nurture yourself through daily care of your body-mind-spirit needs. That means caring for your body through good nutrition and hydration, adequate sleep, exercise, and healthy intimacies and relationships with others.

Self-love demands that you protect yourself from harmful energies of those who do not respect your boundaries. To cultivate caring toward yourself, forgive and let go of guilt. You don't benefit from having guilt in your life, and being hard on yourself won't further your happiness or success. Love yourself and live an intentional life on purpose with your deepest dreams and desires. Make it a ritual to rise each day and affirm that this is a new day, full of possibilities. Claim it as yours.

Stop Doubting Yourself

Think of doubt as streaks on a window. They can create an unpleasant distraction from what you're trying to see outside. Doubts have the same effect on your energy—they distract it and make it congested. When you begin to doubt yourself, tell yourself, *Now that courage, strength, and love are in motion, all shadows of doubt are erased.*

Similar to wiping a window clean, use this mantra to transform doubt into courage and happiness. It's best to sit or stand up tall when you're reciting it. Allow yourself to really feel the mantra in your body.

◆

Being happy
isn't having
everything in your
life be perfect.
Maybe it's about
stringing together
all the little things.

—ANN BRASHARES
American author

Follow the 60 Percent Rule

Perfection isn't possible. But many people pursue perfectionism with such vigor that it can actually be damaging. It's time to readjust that thinking. According to the 60 percent rule, if your friendships, work life, and relationships are 60 percent "perfect," then you are doing something right. Keep up the good work! Pushing for perfectionism will cause you unneeded stress and anxiety—instead, embrace the imperfect and feel happier.

Move Past Perfection

If you love to get things right every time and invest in high standards and lofty goals, falling short isn't an option. But when it happens, the voice of your inner critic might sound off loud and clear. Worse, that self-critical voice can be unrelenting, torturing you for days afterward. You might feel anger, guilt, and a whole lot of frustration at not finishing something or seeing it turn out less than perfectly. Letting go of the need for perfection might seem almost impossible until you figure out how to tamp down the inner critic and move past the need to control to feel happy again. Once you can move past that compulsion, you open space in your being to feel joy.

Light a candle scented with sweet orange, a scent favored in Europe, Arabia, and China during the tenth century to foster relaxation and warm, comforting, and peaceful feelings. Deep breathe for six breaths and then relax and focus your thoughts on things that you can do successfully rather than perfectly, which is so much easier. Repeat this process until you feel peace settle in your bones.

See Beyond Your Thoughts

Go beyond your thoughts. Your thoughts could never capture the possibilities and magnificence that are available to you when you allow yourself to move through your feelings and detach from thinking.

Tell yourself, *It's got to be better than I think*. Reciting this mantra opens the doorway to new ways of being, and as this occurs new perceptions will surface. Sensations create perceptions. Utilizing this mantra gives you a much more open feeling, providing an inevitable shift in the way you see your world.

✦

Success is not
the key to happiness.
Happiness is the key
to success. If you love
what you are doing,
you will be successful.

—ALBERT SCHWEITZER
German theologian, philosopher, and physician

Celebrate with Bubbly

Even if you don't have a special occasion like an anniversary or birthday to celebrate, break out a good bottle of bubbly (nonalcoholic works just as well) and a fancy champagne flute. To make it even more special, put a strawberry in the drink. You can do this by yourself or with a loved one. Give a toast to honor something you are proud of or happy about today. A little sense of occasion on an otherwise boring night will make you feel special. Don't forget that just waking up in the morning is a reason to celebrate.

Organize a Group

A quick way to turn your life around and move in a happier direction is to focus on your passion. Involving others means you'll keep your attention on the work of the organization and stay focused. If some life event has sparked your passion for something—be it clean air or water, animal rights, human rights, eco-travel, organic winemaking, or something else—consider how you might create a movement or at least an organization to promote interest in your idea. Upon awakening, when your mind is refreshed from sleep, set aside time to do some mindful breathing.

Begin meditating on ideas for a new life direction. Focus on what speaks powerfully to your heart. Can you develop a vision for a long-range project that addresses your strongest passion? If so, what might be some of the action steps to create an organization that addresses your keen interest? Write down your ideas in a journal. Focus on the meaning they bring to your life and why you'd want to spend weeks, months, even years involved in the work of a group that shares your zeal. When you feel your head and heart are aligned around your vision, write out the steps and begin to actualize it.

Trust Your Path

There is no right or wrong path. All paths lead to the heart. Live in love and happiness and your path will be illuminated for you. Like most paths, don't be surprised if there are twists and turns filled with unhappiness. Stay focused on the moment and repeat this mantra: *Uncertainty awakens me now. I trust this path.* State the mantra when you start to second-guess your decisions or question your capabilities. It's not that you won't change your mind from time to time, but maintain trust that the path unfolding for you has its source in the eternal flow of life.

✦

If you want to
be happy, set a goal
that commands your
thoughts, liberates
your energy, and
inspires your hopes.

—ANDREW CARNEGIE
American industrialist and philanthropist

Make a Ten-Point List of What's Really Important to You

Millions of people live their lives without a sense of direction. Unless you know what's really important to you and what you want out of life, how are you going to know where you are going, how to get what you want, and what your life purpose is? Think of ten things that are most important to you (for example, family unity). Then make each item as specific as possible. Instead of *family unity*, maybe you really mean *eating meals together*, *working on the chores together*, or *praying together*. Refine the ten things on your list until you know exactly what is of primary importance to you. These are the things that will make you happiest. Knowing what they are can help you make better choices in your personal life journey.

Ask for Something

Whether it's asking a family member to pass a napkin, a friend for a favor, or your husband to take the kids so you can go to yoga, challenge yourself to open your mouth and make a request today. This is related to, but different from, asking yourself what you most need in this moment—it's taking the insight you gain from a moment of reflection and saying it out loud. Making such a request takes awareness. It also takes allowing yourself to be seen as having needs. Which means it can also take courage (especially if you are an "I can handle it" type). But speaking up will bring you comfort and empowerment.

Choose Love

Overfocusing on your problems or worrying about the future disables your ability to tune in to love and happiness. If you question your relationships or expect that certain things in your life are unlikely to work out, then you'll strip away at the love inside of you. Rather than continue these patterns, choose to focus on self-love by telling yourself, *Choosing to love myself comes more easily now. I am learning to listen to the needs of my body and spirit.*

Self-love is not as complicated or overwhelming as you might think. The act of pausing and taking a drink of water is a demonstration of love. Noticing the temperature of the water as it runs over your hands while washing dishes is a way to connect to love. Love is in the moment; it is right now, as you are reading this. It is recognizing the happiness all around you and celebrating that happiness. Pay attention to how your body responds to the experiences and interactions of your day without judgment. Soak up moments that offer you connections to the moment. These are all part of love.

✦

Happiness consists more in small conveniences or pleasures that occur every day, than in great pieces of good fortune that happen but seldom.

—BENJAMIN FRANKLIN
American Founding Father

Listen to Music and Sing Along

Have you ever noticed how good you feel when you hear certain songs or how an old tune can bring back a flood of happy memories? That's because music is a mood enhancer. Listening to music releases serotonin (our favorite feel-good hormone) into your system and makes you feel happy. In addition, singing a song triggers a tiny organ in your inner ear called the saccule. It's connected to a part of your brain that registers pleasure, making you feel good no matter how good of a singer you are!

Do Deep Breathing

From the moment you awaken your mind begins chattering with a steady stream of thoughts. Establish a positive mental state by counting a cycle of deep and slow breaths for five minutes or more. Make the count of your exhalation twice as long as the inhalation. Mindful breath work is a surefire way to calm the noise in your mind, slow the mental babble, and center your thoughts. Deep breathing can be done anytime during the day when you have a free minute or two. Before an early-morning ritual of breath work, note the following:

- Avoid eating for several hours (easy when you do your practice upon awakening).
- Drink only water one half-hour before practice.
- Wear loose clothes.
- Align your head and spine for correct posture.

Eating and drinking can cause stomach upset and you don't want your clothes to bind you as you practice deep breathing. Deep breathing detoxifies your body and oxygenates your cells while easing away stress and tension. It strengthens the lungs, heart, and immune system and also elevates mood, boosts stamina, and generates mental acuity.

Walk Away from Drama

Interpersonal drama is created from conflict, insecurity, and pain. Perhaps you live in a family where gossip and conflict are common. Or maybe your workplace environment is like this. These types of family and/or work dynamics can get quite heated with tension. In an attempt to cope with the situation, you may be forced to detach yourself from it all. This may work to some degree, but tuning out or walking away is only a part of the process. As you walk away, remind yourself that you are *Neutralizing drama now* by uttering that phrase to yourself. See yourself as becoming neutral to what is happening. This means the drama does not impact you either way. In other words, you are able to observe without being drawn in.

◆

Even a happy life cannot be without a measure of darkness, and the word happy would lose its meaning if it were not balanced by sadness. It is far better to take things as they come along with patience and equanimity.

—CARL JUNG
Swiss psychiatrist

Don't Be Unhappy
about Being Unhappy

There is pain in life. At some point in your glorious life, you will be unhappy, hurt, or depressed. These things are natural and are part of everyone's human experience. The most important thing during these times is to not beat yourself up about feeling the way you do. Feeling bad or embarrassed about feeling bad will not help you; in fact, those additional negative feelings may just drag you down even further. Instead, acknowledge your feelings—they are nothing to be ashamed of. Accepting the pain and difficulty of a situation is one of the ways to help yourself get out of it and back on the path to happiness.

Be the Light in the Darkness

When faced with darkness, become a beacon of light. Be an exemplar of humility, civility, patience, compassion, kindness, sincerity, and—above all—calmness. Acting with positive energy doesn't just make other people happy. It makes you happy too! You might even make a few friends along the way.

1. Sit with a straight spine. Close your eyes and tune in to your heart as you breathe naturally in a slow pattern.
2. Visualize a beautiful temple. See yourself crossing a peaceful lake that washes away all negativity as you prepare to enter the temple.
3. Let the temple light embrace you as the inner sound of tinkling bells rings out your presence.
4. Call forth an individual with whom you've had a negative encounter.
5. Welcome him or her into the temple's sacred space.
6. Observe how the darkness dissipates once you act with compassion.
7. Fix your thoughts on the good in all hearts.
8. Rest in the healing light of friendship.

Shine in the Light

The lighter you are, the more aware you become and the more happiness you'll be able to embody. Emotions such as guilt and shame bog you down, making you feel heavy. Guilt and shame don't stand a chance when you expose them to light. The key is to become aware enough so that you are able to recognize when these emotions are transforming into symptoms such as tightness in your body. When you feel these emotions creep up, simply proclaim to yourself, *I am light!* This is important because tightness restricts your ability to breathe. Shallow breathing interferes with your ability to truly read and listen to your body's wisdom. See this mantra as a way to invite more light into your body.

✦

It is not how
much we have,
but how much
we enjoy, that
makes happiness.

—CHARLES SPURGEON
Nineteenth-century English preacher and author

Eat Your Favorite Food

You know how happy you feel when you're eating your favorite food. That's why it's your favorite. Cook or order that one dish that just puts a smile on your face. It could be comfort food from your childhood, an exotic creation you first tasted on vacation, or even a savory palate-pleaser you learned to cook when you were dating someone from another country. Happily savor every bite of that Moroccan chicken tagine, New England crab cake, Midwestern meatloaf, Southern fried chicken, or whatever is your favorite.

✦

If you spend your whole life waiting for the storm, you'll never enjoy the sunshine.

—MORRIS WEST
Australian author

Sniff a Memory

The connection between scent and memory begins before you're even born and develops as you grow. Your nose learns to detect thousands of scents and to associate certain odors with special memories. Two olfactory receptors in your nasal passages carry odors to the limbic system (the ancient, primitive part of the brain believed to be the seat of emotion). You may respond emotionally to a scent even before you can recognize and name it. Odors that bring up pleasant memories lift your mood and foster happiness, which contributes to good health, enhances creativity, and boosts problem-solving abilities.

Keep a vial of essential oil at the ready that you associate with a pleasant personal memory or choose lemon (for cheerfulness), lavender (for stress-relieving clarity), and rosemary (for energy). On a facecloth folded in half and then half again, place a drop or two on the top fold.

1. Close your eyes.
2. Hold the scented cloth under your nose.
3. Allow a fond memory to rise in your thoughts.
4. Inhale gently to the count of four.
5. Hold to the count of four.
6. Exhale to the count of eight and repeat at least three times.

Use this ritual anytime you feel the need to return to a happier emotional state.

Free Yourself from Collective Consciousness

Many things divide us from oneness: religion, politics, and cultural viewpoints. Having the freedom to choose your religion and vote for whom you believe would best serve your country is a privilege. However, if you find yourself getting caught up in collective belief systems that foster negativity, anger, and even hate, you may begin to feel the negative impact of this collective consciousness. Remind yourself to avoid these systems by telling yourself, *I release all unforgiving thoughts supported by the collective consciousness.* This is not to say unity isn't important, but respecting differences is critical to our evolution. This mantra helps you release that negativity.

If you want happiness for an hour, take a nap. If you want happiness for a day, go fishing. If you want happiness for a year, inherit a fortune. If you want happiness for a lifetime, help someone else.

—CHINESE PRVERB

Memorize a Funny Joke and Share It

Heard any good jokes lately? Have you tried passing them on? Telling a funny joke is a terrific way to cheer up others, defuse tense situations, add much-needed levity in times of stress, and generate some positive effects on your health. Memorizing a joke and telling it to others is just one way to cultivate a sense of humor. Did you know that laughing may actually reduce your risk for heart disease and can mitigate damage incurred when you are experiencing deep distress and pain? Also, some sources say that while sniffles, sneezes, and coughing are contagious, laughter is more so. Want to feel good? Be able to laugh at stressful situations. Did you hear the one about…?

Analyze Intentions Behind Your Gift

When you are the recipient of a good turn by others, take time to think about what in their hearts led them to give you that gift. Think about the motivation of the gift giver and the timing. You might realize that the decision of the gift giver wasn't entirely whimsical but perhaps purposeful. You were chosen to receive for a reason—he or she wanted to bring you happiness.

Ask yourself what the person had to pay to give you that gift, either in money or time. For example, if your gift was a jar of jam from the first ripe batch of apricots on your neighbor's tree, think about how much time your neighbor spent gathering, washing, pitting, and peeling the apricots, mixing the fruit with other ingredients, stirring the pot, filling and processing the jars. This likely will bring a sense of deep appreciation. Pour yourself a cup of tea and put your feet up. Reflect on the person who has done you a good turn. Sip your tea and come up with several ways you could repay the kindness. Act on one of them.

Recognize Your Support

If you rarely ask for help and tend to take the world on your shoulders, you might want to consider getting to know this mantra. Always going it alone can be incredibly stressful and can lead to a lot of unhappiness in your life. Taking on the worries and concerns without regard for yourself makes life seem heavy and challenging, rather than light and interesting. If you believe you are unsupported, change your thinking by saying, *The universe generously supports me.* The universe will reflect that back to you. Realizing that you have the support of more than just the things and people around you can alleviate much of your stress and unhappiness. You also have universal support—in many ways a spiritual team—that you can access through mantras.

Learn to enjoy every
minute of your life.
Be happy now. Don't wait
for something outside
of yourself to make you
happy in the future.
Think how really pre-
cious is the time you have
to spend, whether it's at
work or with your family.
Every minute should be
enjoyed and savored.

—EARL NIGHTINGALE
American motivational speaker and author

Try After-Dinner Gratitude

Each night after dinner, write down five good things that happened to you during the day. Most people are tired after a long day at work and can tend to drift toward the negative, but by doing this exercise, you can redirect your mood toward the things that are going well and thus increase your positivity. Pause for a few minutes to write down the things that went just the way you'd planned or perhaps some small surprises during the day that put a smile on your face. Writing down these gratitudes may sound trivial, but journaling this way has been proven to reduce stress and redirect people out of negative cycles.

Kick Off Your Shoes and Get Going

When you've had a long, stressful day at work and are facing an evening of chores such as preparing dinner, doing laundry, and helping the kids with homework, you might not feel like exercising. However, exercise is just what you need to release the stress and find your happiness. Thirty minutes of walking, working out in a gym, or doing tai chi can stimulate chemicals in your brain to help you feel reinvigorated, relaxed, and happier. If you hate the idea of exercising alone, look for a group workout opportunity earlier in the day. Join a dance troupe or a swim or soccer team.

Exercise improves your energy, stamina, sex life, cardiovascular health, and helps with weight loss while also reducing your risk for chronic diseases such as depression, type 2 diabetes, arthritis, certain cancers, and metabolic syndrome. Aim for thirty minutes of daily exercise five days each week. As your stamina improves, lengthen your workout period. You'll discover it boosts your overall happiness as well as your thinking power, confidence, self-esteem, and bone health. Sit quietly after exercise and feel your pulse pounding, your heart beating, and your lungs rhythmically inhaling and exhaling. Feel gratitude and give thanks for the energy that supports your healthy body as well as the universe.

Allow Yourself to Receive

You cannot receive what you don't allow. In fact, allowing is a pre-requisite for receiving. In order to become more open to what the universe has to offer, give yourself permission to release any fear of making a mistake. Allow yourself to receive happiness by saying, *I am open to what the universe has to offer*. When you fear making a mistake, that fear is likely holding you back from trying something new. As you recite this mantra, close your eyes and imagine an open door or window. Allow yourself to feel the happiness moving in and out of the opening.

We tend to
forget that happiness
doesn't come as a
result of getting
something we don't
have, but rather
of recognizing and
appreciating what
we do have.

—FRIEDRICH KOENIG
German inventor

Get a Bestie Massage

Let your best friend know how much you value her friendship by inviting her along for a relaxing afternoon at the spa. Treat her to her favorite relaxation treatment or a hot stone massage. Imagine how great she'll feel when the massage therapist places warm stones of smooth volcanic rock on her tired back, shoulders, and neck muscles. If there's been any friction between you, a spa day can ease that as well. Go ahead and book that appointment! Invest some time and cost in your friendship—a happy relationship with your best friend is worth every penny.

Visualize Friendship

Friends are essential to true happiness. No one can walk through life alone and expect to be happy. Examine your life for the friends who helped you in some way to blossom. Express why you appreciate someone who has touched your life in profound and positive ways in an act of gratitude. Send out joy and appreciation and they will return to bless you.

1. Find a comfortable position in a chair or on a mat. Sit erect with eyes closed.
2. Take several deep, cleansing breaths.
3. Mentally invite in the friends who are walking with you on this journey of life—people who've touched you in a special way.
4. Focus on each person, explaining his or her particular gift to you and why you view it as a blessing.
5. Elaborate on how the blessing affects your life today.
6. Visualize the next friend and repeat the process. Do this until you've addressed each, in turn.
7. Thank your friends; vow to write a note of appreciation to each during the week (and follow through on that promise).
8. Rest in the warm happy feelings of being valued by your special coterie of friends. As you go forth into your day, do good for others as your friends have done for you.

Accept All That Comes Your Way

I love you, I am sorry, please forgive me, thank you. This Hawaiian chant (a *Ho'oponopono* prayer chant) is an especially powerful one. When reciting this chant, you are taking full responsibility for everything that comes your way. Only by accepting everything can you be truly happy no matter what comes.

This chant speaks to karma and how things in this life may show up due to karma in a former life. Do your best to follow the traditional mantra frequency recommendation with this one: that is, try to repeat it 108 times daily for forty days. You will benefit if you do it less, but if you are experiencing difficult circumstances or have people in your life with a lot of problems, you may want to do the full 108 times.

If you look to others for fulfillment, you will never be fulfilled. If your happiness depends on money, you will never be happy with yourself. Be content with what you have; rejoice in the way things are. When you realize there is nothing lacking, the world belongs to you.

—LAO TZU
Chinese philosopher and founder of Taoism

Realize That Happiness Comes from Within

Often people pin their hopes on external conditions that are out of their control, or they underestimate their power to control their own happiness. Never forget the power of the mind to generate happiness! The mind can make you feel miserable even if you're living in paradise, or the mind can make you feel happy even in the midst of adversity. Make your mind your best friend rather than your enemy, and happiness will follow.

Make Note of Small Pleasures

Appreciation is a form of loving attention, and it creates an uplifting state of happiness that we don't tend to spend much time in. Build your appreciation muscles by taking note of five small things—things you might not otherwise notice—that you appreciate.

In a notebook, number a list 1 to 5. Then, throughout the day, fill each line with one thing that makes your life better—the friend who leaves a funny comment on your *Instagram*, the sneeze that clears your sinuses, the scent of your neighbor's barbecue, the way your child instinctively reaches for your hand as you walk down the street.

Make writing this ritual a daily check-in for three weeks—about how long it takes to establish a new habit. The more you make note of the things you value, the more things you'll find to appreciate.

Take a "Me" Day

There are many things we celebrate in life: babies, milestones, birthdays, etc. Every once in a while, though, it's important to take the time to say, *I'm celebrating me today*. This mantra reminds you to acknowledge your growth, even the little things. You work hard and deserve to reward yourself with your very own special occasion day. So shut off your phone and spend some time assessing and appreciating where you're at. Today, celebrate your strengths and your willingness to forgive yourself and others. See the honor and courage required in these actions.

✦

Happiness
is holding
someone in your
arms and knowing
you hold the
whole world.

—ORHAN PAMUK
Turkish author and winner of the 2006 Nobel Prize in Literature

Do Crafts with Kids

Get out the box of craft supplies and create something fun, whimsical, or beautiful with some kids in your life. Quality time with children is never time wasted—it's fun for all, and the attention of grownups makes the kids feel loved and wanted. And it sure beats sitting in front of the TV.

Set aside an hour to work on a project. Share your favorite crafting activity with the kids, or learn a new craft together. It doesn't have to be anything fancy; the kids will appreciate your investment of time in them, no matter what you're doing. Your creative pursuits will make you and the kids happy; plus, you might end up with some personalized art to keep for yourself.

Slip Away for a Couples Retreat

Putting the spark back into your relationship with your spouse can feel like a new beginning. Longtime couples all too often fall into a rut while dealing with day-to-day domestic life over the years; communication and relationship work can take a back seat to other time commitments. Taking time away, just the two of you, can help rekindle the feelings that drew you to each other in the first place.

Plan a long weekend or weeklong retreat where you two are captive audiences for each other. On the retreat, undertake the following suggested steps as a daily ritual: First, hold hands, walk and talk, and freely express your most intimate selves to each other. Go fishing or ride horseback or do some other fun activity. Doing fun things together can facilitate communication. Pledge your desire to draw closer and formulate a plan with your partner for how the two of you will do that. Talk about your plan again before bed. Promise each other that going forward you'll make efforts to ensure that your relationship remains a priority.

Move Forward Along the Parenting Path

Your parenting journey will be anything but perfect. In fact, you'll be on a journey that's often marked by imperfections. You may often feel unhappy where you are along the parenting path. Everything you once knew changes. Suddenly that nice clean white shirt you have worn for years doesn't quite fit the same, and it also has spit-up stains on it. Outward appearances are not the only thing that changes. Finances, schedules, and your sex life also become upended. Let go of attempting to hold on to what once was and say, *I am the light of perfection. My baby is the light of perfection. Our family is the light of perfection now*. This mantra encourages you to replace perfection with presence. Put your attention on your light and know you are on a well-traveled journey.

♦

It's the moments
that I stopped
just to be,
rather than do,
that have given me
true happiness.

—RICHARD BRANSON
English entrepreneur

Spend a Day Alone

"Me time" is a concept that is slowly slipping away in our hectic world, but it's critical for your mental health. For just one day, try to spend that day with only yourself—no family, no friends, no coworkers. While these people may have your best intentions in mind, they are often a distraction from getting to know your real self. Spend a day relaxing, doing the things you love, eating foods that make you happy, and focusing on you and your purpose. Avoid checking your phone at all. Really unplug yourself from the world. It won't be as awful as you may think! In fact, the peace that comes from occasional solitude will make you feel refreshed and calm.

Walk with No Destination

Here's a way to get some movement while also building your relationship with your intuition, and keeping this relationship strong is vital to your happiness. At some point each week, take yourself on a walk with no particular destination in mind. Every time you come to a crossroads, take a look in each direction and head the way that's calling to you the most. You're not trying to get anywhere—you're simply letting your gut lead the way. This exercise is a tangible way to reprogram the well-worn paths of your thoughts, and can open you up to delightful surprises—a coffee shop you've never noticed before, for example, or a chance encounter with a dog or a neighbor who's not on your usual route.

Breathe Deep for Happiness

When you're feeling stressed and unhappy, take a moment to repeat the simplest of mantras: *Ahhhhh*. This simple sound is far more powerful than you may think. You're giving yourself permission to release that pain in your neck (or anywhere else!) and return to being happy. Muscle tension is often a reflection of energy that is being held hostage in the body. As a result, the body becomes depleted of oxygen. Circulating fresh oxygen deep into your body helps you release this pent-up energy. Go ahead, fill up your belly with breath. Inflate it now, fully (like a balloon). Allow your mouth to open slightly and release a nice *Ahhhhh* sound.

✦

Dream as if
you'll live forever,
live as if you'll
die today.

—JAMES DEAN
American actor

Daydream for Twenty Minutes Every Morning

Daydreaming can stimulate your mind in creative ways, reduce stress, elevate your mood, organize your thinking, stimulate ideas for solutions to problems, and help you gain new perspectives on troubling issues. Assuming that you are not using daydreams to escape from being fully engaged in your life or to retreat from your responsibilities, then a regular period of daydreaming is not only healthy but helpful in solving problems and fostering creativity. Set a timer. Let your thoughts take flight to a Greek island, a trekking path high in the Himalayas, a manicured estate in England, a beach in Barbados, or somewhere else; indulge yourself. Let your thoughts take flight.

Have More Fun

You can't be having fun and feeling stressed at the same time—fun is light, enjoyable, and energizing. It broadens your horizons, where stress is depleting and limits your focus to that which is urgent. So...how much fun have you been having lately? If the answer is none, or not enough, look at your calendar for the next week and find a time to do at least one thing just for recreation—play tennis with a friend, go salsa dancing, visit a used bookstore. Having it scheduled will help you relax a little the rest of the week, knowing that you're doing something to tend to your happiness. Also, encourage yourself to weave smaller bits of fun into your everyday experience—eat dinner on the patio, drive home the pretty way, play with the kids on the playground instead of checking your phone. These moments will lift your spirits and make everything else you do feel a little more effortless.

Release Your Resistance

Have you heard the phrase, "What you resist persists"? In other words, if you resist feeling free and happy by holding on to negative emotions, your body will learn how to remain in a state of resistance. This is fine if you are truly being threatened, but you are not meant to be in a state of resistance for very long. Free yourself of this resistance by announcing, *All resistance melt freely from me now.* As you recite this mantra, see resistance melting, kind of like an ice-cream cone on a hot day or a Popsicle in the sun.

✦

Happiness
is not a state
to arrive at,
but a manner
of traveling.

—MARGARET LEE RUNBECK
American author

Drink Wine with Friends

If you and your friends enjoy wine, consider forming a wine club. (A club where you get to drink is one of the best kinds!) Host monthly meetings where you have blind tastings. Here's how you do it:

1. Before each meeting, decide on one type of wine you'll taste that session: Pinot (Noir or Gris), Cabernet Sauvignon, Burgundy, Chardonnay, Sauvignon Blanc, Zinfandel, or whatever you like.
2. Have each person bring a bottle of the selected type of wine and one appetizer to share with everyone. (If you're going to be drinking all that wine, you'll want some food in your stomach too!)
3. Wrap each bottle in a numbered paper bag so that no one can see the label (and possibly form a bias), then give everyone pencils and notecards and have them write down their comments about each bottle they taste. Let the adventure begin!

You may discover a new favorite wine. At the very least, you'll have a great time trying something new with your friends.

Find Peace During Uncertainty

Because life is dynamic, it's unpredictable and uncertain. Some people adapt easier than others to change. When the turbulence of not knowing forces you outside your comfort zone, you might feel anxiety, distress, and fear. In meditation you can sense the steadiness underlying all uncertainty and find refuge and joy therein. All change provides opportunities to move in new directions, gain a new perspective as you view the world through a different lens, and find unique gifts that change calls forth in you.

1. Sit cross-legged on your yoga mat or in a chair with your feet flat on the floor, palms cradling a small elephant carved from agate or another earth stone, ideas of stability and constancy in your thoughts. (In some cultures of the world, nothing symbolizes strength and stability like the elephant.)
2. Close your eyes and visualize your root chakra (Muladhara) as a spinning red wheel at the base of your spine.
3. Imagine an energy ray in a continuous loop as it flows from your root chakra to pierce deep into the earth's core and return to your chakra.
4. Chant *Lam* (the sound that is traditionally connected to the root chakra) to energize your root chakra as you meditate on peace.

Stay Calm in Your Car

If you spend a good amount of time traveling each day, you know how stressful it can be. Whether you're commuting to and from work or driving your children around town, you encounter noise, traffic, and frustrated people! Sometimes blotting out the noise is a viable option. Block out the road rage by telling yourself, *May I have peace within my heart, peace with all of my relationships, and peace with all beings.*

◆

On the whole,
the happiest people
seem to be those
who have no
particular cause for
being happy except
that they are so.

—WILLIAM R. INGE
English Anglican priest

Play in the Water

There's nothing like playing in the water on a hot summer day. Whether you swim, snorkel, water-ski, deep-sea dive, surf, or head out in a kayak or canoe, there's so much fun to be had in the water! Go buy yourself a bathing suit and join your family or friends for some water play. Of course, be safe: use adequate sunscreen to protect yourself from the sun's harmful rays, wear a hat with a wide brim to shade your face and neck, and avoid the hottest times of the day (when the sun is directly overhead). Also, drink plenty of water to replenish what you sweat away with all that exercise. Now go and have a blast!

Practice Loving-Kindness Toward Yourself

Think of loving-kindness as a feel-good tonic for all the little irritations during the day that disturb your peace. The easiest way to practice loving-kindness of self is through breath work and mantras. By stirring your feelings of happiness toward yourself, you become empowered to radiate that feeling toward others. It's as though you are wrapping them in the warm blanket of joy you've created through your generosity of spirit.

The first step in creating a loving-kindness ritual for peace directed toward yourself might be to come up with a phrase that you can recite mentally or aloud repeatedly throughout your day. The *Peace be with you* phrase used in some religious services is succinct and powerful. Or you might say on the inhaled breath, *May I live in peace*. On the exhaled breath, you might say, *May peace permeate my being*. Use myrrh aromatherapy in a diffuser or warmed wax burner to link your chosen phrase with a scent that will always remind you to recite those words.

Move In, Not On

When it comes to forgiveness, there is no moving on; there is only moving in. Your attitude and life experiences may change, but it is only when you move deeper into yourself that you will truly be liberated. The next time you hear yourself saying, "I need to move on" or "If only I could just stop thinking about this person or situation," consider reciting *I choose to let go by moving in rather than moving on.*

Allow this mantra to draw your awareness inward. As you move inward, your perception will shift and you may realize that there was never anything to let go of in the first place. The thing you thought you needed to let go of turns into something you have learned to appreciate and respect.

✦

Sometimes your
joy is the source
of your smile,
but sometimes your
smile can be the
source of your joy.

—THICH NHAT HANH
Buddhist monk and author

Read a Funny Book to a Kid

If you love to read, spend some time reading to children. You can read books to kids anywhere: at home, at a local library, at an infant and toddler daycare center, at a nursery school, in a doctor's or dentist's waiting room, in a hospital waiting room, or even at kids' organizations like the Cub Scouts or Brownies. Just be sure that your book is appropriate for the age group. A funny book will inspire laughter, and you'll likely laugh too—the happy laughter of children is infectious.

Ask Three Friends to Kidnap You

If you've ever had a friend show up unexpectedly and whisk you away for an afternoon of fun, you know how refreshed, exhilarated, and renewed that can make you feel. Why wait for your friends to get the idea that you need a break from the doldrums of your daily grind? Call them up and explain this is your plan to feel renewed. Maybe one or more of them also needs a break. Go wine-tasting or catch the latest artsy film at the local theater. Take a picnic lunch to the beach or pack up some sandwiches and water and head out to a farm to pick local produce. If crafting is your thing, ask your friends to sign up the group at a local pottery shop or take a bead-making class together.

If you enjoy your day, why not make it a monthly foray into the unknown? Let each friend choose a secret destination and activity each month. To stimulate your creative imagination for other ideas of fun outings, put on some happy music. Get out a notebook. Jot down your name along with your friends'. Beneath each one, list activities you know they love to do.

Accept the Emotional Pain

Anxiety and depression can hurt. Not only do they give you emotional symptoms such as nervousness and sadness, they also show up as physical symptoms such as neck pain, fatigue, and backache. Hiding these feelings may hinder your healing potential and hamper your happiness more than they already do. When you're struggling with these terrible diseases, remind yourself that "You have to feel it to heal it." To feel means to give yourself permission to experience an emotion (e.g., worry) from beginning, middle, to end.

The best way to do this is through mindful breathing. One simple tip is to actually count as you breathe (as you inhale and exhale). To do that, inflate your belly to the count of three, and on exhale deflate your lower abdomen to the count of three. At first it may seem awkward, but with practice you'll begin to experience the power of mind-body healing.

✦

"What day is it?"
asked Winnie
the Pooh.

"It's today,"
squeaked Piglet.

"My favorite day,"
said Pooh.

—A.A. MILNE
English author

Get at Least Eight Hours
of Sleep Each Night

If you want to wake up happy with a hopeful, positive outlook, get adequate sleep. Your body needs it. Without sufficient sleep, sleep researchers say, your mental function becomes impaired. Certain regulatory systems and important organs continue their vital work while you sleep. Researchers have been able to pinpoint parts of the brain that actually increase their activities when subjects are asleep. Inadequate sleep has serious consequences. For example, it can negatively impact your daytime performance, causing lower levels of energy and duller thinking. Adequate sleep, however, enables you to wake up refreshed, energized, and in a good mood.

Savor Better Sleep

You may need six to nine hours of good sleep nightly, but are you getting it? Clearing away the chaos of the day isn't always easy. Sometimes just getting to sleep proves difficult. But sleep is how the body and brain heal and cells renew. Yoga nidra ("yogic sleep") involves deep conscious relaxation to release muscle tension and emotions trapped in your subconscious after a hectic day. Do yoga nidra as your body hits those cool cotton sheets. Deep, restorative sleep will soon engulf you.

1. Lie in the Corpse Pose (*Savasana*).
2. Focus your attention on the right foot and ankle.
3. Move your attention slowly up the whole limb. Relax it.
4. Repeat the process for the left lower limb.
5. Mentally check in with your pelvis, tummy, and torso.
6. Shift your attention to your right shoulder and guide your attention along the arm down to your hand and fingers. Feel the whole limb relax.
7. Repeat step 6 for the left shoulder, arm, and hand.
8. Breathe in, breathe out with an awareness of all the sensations in your body.
9. Turn onto your right side, where left-nostril breathing cools your body (lying on your right side means the left nostril is higher than the right and air flows easily and without restriction through the left). Relax.
10. Roll onto your back. Deepen the relaxation until you cross the threshold into restorative sleep.

Rest Up

It's not uncommon to have days where you feel wiped out or drained. You might have to put in extra hours at work, for example. Or perhaps you had too little sleep due to nursing a new baby. If these draining days persist, you might start thinking that this is a normal way to live. But it's not, and your health and happiness will eventually suffer from the long-term stress.

Whenever you start to fade or feel run-down, regain your normal, well-rested form by reciting the mantra, *I bounce back easily*. This mantra helps you shake off wearying thoughts so that you can get right back on your feet. Be sure to give yourself permission to rest, and also drink plenty of water. Close your eyes, pause, and allow the energy to rest inside of you.

✦

To be kind to all,
to like many and
love a few, to be
needed and wanted
by those we love,
is certainly the
nearest we can
come to happiness.

—MARY STUART
Former queen of Scotland

Throw Your Own Birthday Bash

Instead of having the usual dinner with your significant other or relatives, why not plan a birthday bash that you'll never forget? Perhaps you want to fly to London to shop at Harrods and then go to the theater district to see a play. What are you waiting for? Book the trip. You only live once. Or maybe you've always wanted to go mountain climbing or scuba diving or skydiving. Get on the internet, find out what's involved, and do it. Whatever you do, do it your way and enjoy every minute of it.

Keep a Gratitude Journal

When you want to focus on the positives in your life, a gratitude journal can be a powerful tool. Scientific evidence supports the notion that people who are grateful tend to be happier than those who aren't. When you focus on happiness-boosting activities that include random acts of kindness you do for others, it enhances your levels of gratitude.

Maintaining such a journal can lead to greater optimism as you count your blessings. Write in the journal at least once weekly. Write three things for which you feel grateful or bring you joy. Add other positive observations and jot down inspiring quotes or happiness goals. Create a title for that day's entries. Look up gratitude affirmations or inspiring quotes on your computer and print them for inclusion in your journal. As the weeks progress, you can look back over your entries and feel uplifted and fulfilled by all the goodness in your life.

Foster Your Sense of Belonging

By nature, human beings need to feel connected to others. This connection is a necessary daily supplement to fostering happiness and growth. Strengthen this sense of belonging by chanting, *I am a part of something greater. My breath unites me with this now.*

Naturally, there may be times when you question how and in what ways you fit in. Perhaps you are a new mom, a student, or newly retired. This uneasiness can even happen within your own family unit. Wanting and trying to fit in or feeling bad for being different often makes things worse. Instead, know that you are always a key part of the universe. You are wanted and needed. This mantra reminds you that you are part of something greater. It connects you to your wholeness (by saying *I am*).

✦

When one door
of happiness closes,
another opens;
but often we look so
long at the closed
door that we do not
see the one that has
been opened for us.

—HELEN KELLER
American activist and author

Don't Dwell

The past is a valuable thing: it holds valuable memories and teaches us lessons. Learn from those lessons and learn from those mistakes…and then let them go. If something bad has happened, see it as an opportunity to learn something you didn't know. If someone else made a mistake, see it as an opportunity to be forgiving and understanding. The past does not define you. Think of the past as practice and training, letting you learn lessons so that you don't repeat them. Don't dwell on the bad aspects of the past and don't live in the pain of old hurts. Move forward!

Find Hope in a New Day

Start your day with the energy and light from the sun. When you start your day with the Salutation to the Sun, its rays of infinite warmth, light, and happiness fill you with happiness and possibility. The full salutation consists of a series of yoga postures, each with an accompanying mantra. What follows is one commonly used as the first position.

1. Rise to face the dawn. Wear loose clothing. Stand with your feet together.
2. Join your hands in prayer at your heart, the pose of respect (*Pranamasana*).
3. Chant the first mantra: *Om Mitraya Namaha*.
4. Continue with yoga poses that generate heat while strengthening your core, or choose to rest for ten minutes before doing a sitting meditation.
5. Close your eyes. Imagine warmth and light permeating your being.
6. Imagine sunlight revitalizing all your cells, restoring them to perfection as the light becomes expansive, spreading throughout your body.
7. Feel saturated with happiness and confidence that what you hope to accomplish will be easier having started your day with the sun.

Create Energy Through Forgiveness

Holding on to old grudges can be one of the most harmful things you can do to yourself. It restricts your energy flow and stops your happiness. Flip these grudges around by offering forgiveness instead of resentment or hatred.

Forgiveness is one of the most powerful ways to gain energy. Think of it as putting on an oxygen mask in a depressurized environment. At first it might feel awkward or even nerve-racking, but once the oxygen starts flowing, you feel alert, replenished, and free. Remind yourself of this power by telling yourself, *I now have the energy and strength to create new thoughts and beliefs.* See this mantra as a way to lift your energy either before or after you practice forgiveness. Without it, you may find yourself falling back into your old ways of seeing things.

✦

Happiness
depends
upon ourselves.

—ARISTOTLE
Ancient Greek philosopher

Take a Spa Day

When you feel like life has become a treadmill and you just need to step off, treat yourself to a day at the spa. Get a manicure, a pedicure, or a skin rejuvenation facial. If you'd like to try something a tad more radical, get a colon cleansing, take a mud bath, or slip into a sensory-deprivation tank. For a healthy state of mind and body, try some treatments at an upscale med-spa center that integrates innovative, cutting-edge therapies and holistic wellness modalities with the ancient healing practices of other cultures.

Enjoy a Five-Minute Renewal

You try to eat well, exercise, and get enough sleep—at least a few hours every night—but sometimes the daily grind doesn't leave much time for self-care. Before *hectic*, *demanding*, *and tiring* becomes the three-word mantra for your life, take a few minutes of each day to rest, relax, and recharge. Listen to your body; it tells you when to stop pushing.

No one can stay at the top of his or her game without some much-needed downtime. Throughout the day, reset your body's batteries by reconnecting with your own source of happiness. Break the busy-busy cycle of work to create breathing space.

1. Sit with a straight spine, palms facing upward on your thighs.
2. Inhale, softly making the sound of *So.*
3. Exhale, making the sound of *Hum.* Do the *So Hum* breathing for one minute. (This mantra, from the Sanskrit, translates as "I am that I am.")
4. Rest your consciousness in the silence for four minutes as your thoughts gravitate toward contact with the Divine.
5. Feel your life-force energy being recharged and reinvigorated and reconnect with your happy place.

Connect to Yourself
Through Your Feelings

So many of us have been taught that our emotions are a sign of weakness or a cue that something might be wrong. This could not be further from the truth. Your emotions are the way you are able to connect with yourself and other human beings. Being in touch with them and acknowledging their power can only bring you happiness. These connections represent true strength and are the ultimate form of protection. Use your feelings to make these connections and tell yourself, *Moving through my feelings brings me joy. I look forward to what is to come.* No one can harm you when you are honest, sincere, and allow yourself to move through (i.e., shed or release) all of your emotions (even the negative ones).

✦

Everyone wants
to live on top of the
mountain, but all
the happiness and
growth occurs while
you're climbing it.

—ANDY ROONEY
American radio and TV writer

Pack Your Pet

Whenever you can steal away for a little rest and relaxation, think about taking your pet with you. Pets bring happiness and love, so why not return the favor and give them a change of scenery and some new experiences?

Traveling with a pet has never been easier—many more hotels, campgrounds, and RV parks are becoming pet-friendly. You might find one at your desired vacation destination by searching DogFriendly.com or Pet-Friendly-Hotels.net or asking other pet owners where they go. If you hesitate to take your dog along on a vacation because he has canine motion sickness, talk with your veterinarian to learn new ways of dealing with that issue. Non-drowsy drugs for motion sickness are available for dogs, for example, or you can take your dog on shorter outings to acclimate him or her to a longer trip.

Don't Just Sit There

Use your chair as a relaxation tool with this simple stretch that also quiets the mind.

1. Scoot to the edge of your seat, opening your feet and knees as wide as the chair seat.
2. Fold forward, resting your torso on your thighs, letting your head and arms dangle down toward the floor.
3. Stay here for a few breaths, feeling your rib cage inflate and deflate with each breath and imagining any stressful thoughts running out of your head and pooling onto the floor.
4. So you don't disturb the peace you just created, roll up out of this slowly.

Find Strength in Yourself

If you're around negativity or feel that someone is taking a lot of energy from you, it's possible that you might react by focusing on an external stressor: a person, situation, phone call, or messy desk. It's kind of like staring at the fuel gauge when your car is running out of gas. As a result, you might get so focused on what you're afraid of that your body starts to go into a fearful state.

If you find yourself in this state, simply remind yourself that, *Moving inward to a place of centeredness strengthens me.* This mantra reminds you to let go of your external surroundings and instead go inward, where your true strength lies. Tune in to your body, breathe, and focus on your feet, skin, and legs. As you do this, your breath will deepen and you will feel completely protected in love.

◆

Action may not always bring happiness; but there is no happiness without action.

—BENJAMIN DISRAELI
Former British prime minister

Stretch

You know how stiff your body feels when you finally get out of a chair after hours of crunching numbers or going through email? Fortunately, it only takes a few minutes to stretch. Some stretches can even be done while sitting in a chair or standing in front of your desk. If you happen to have a yoga mat, take it with you on your break or your lunch hour to a private, peaceful area and do some stretches. You'll feel rejuvenated, flexible, centered, and happier.

Relish the Rainbow

Whether you call the newest healthy food craze a Buddha bowl, hippie bowl, rainbow bowl, or bowl of ancient grains and veggies, it's guaranteed to deliver plenty of balanced nutrition to keep your body and brain healthy and happy. For a lunchtime ritual, create a vitamin- and mineral-packed nourishing bowl of rainbow-colored foods. Include fresh or cooked veggies, fruit, protein, and fat but limit the carbohydrates. Follow these simple steps:

1. Establish a base of colorful, freshly washed leafy greens such as kale, spinach, and a variety of lettuces in a midsized bowl.
2. Add raw veggies such as green broccoli, yellow sweet corn, sliced purplish beets, red onion, orange carrots, beige mushrooms, and white swords of jicama, or cooked vegetables such as green lentils and others of various colors and sizes.
3. Drop in protein-rich ingredients (grilled meat, hard-boiled egg, or tofu).
4. Add a source of healthy fat (fish, avocado, nuts).
5. Sprinkle nuts, seeds, or berries over the top, and toss together if you desire to mix the ingredients.

Stay Active

It can be tempting to scratch exercise off your to-do list. This may be because you see exercise as an activity that takes away your time and energy, rather than as an activity that offers you health and well-being. But the truth is, exercise does not take anything away from you; expectations do. When you're feeling like you just want to sink into your couch and stay there all day, tell yourself, *I say yes to daily activity*. Even if you can't do a killer workout every day, you still can take a flight of stairs rather than an elevator. This mantra encourages you to let go of the sense of obligation (the *I have to*s and the *I haven't been in a while*s). This mantra gives you a boost by encouraging you to say yes to movement.

✦

Optimism is a
happiness magnet.
If you stay positive,
good things and
good people will be
drawn to you.

—MARY LOU RETTON
American gymnast

Anticipate More

Anticipation is often sweeter than the actual experience, particularly when the upcoming event is guaranteed to be pleasurable, such as going out on a romantic date or taking a beach vacation. Anticipating future rewards lights up the pleasure centers in your brain in the same way that experiencing the event does. Think about it: you feel butterflies and grin endlessly an hour before that special date. That's because your brain recognizes all of the pleasant situations leading up to the ultimate reward.

So dream up something that will lead to joyful anticipation! Even if making it happen seems an impossibility, envision what you'd like to happen in minute detail and savor each mental picture. Remember, intensely visualizing something can trick your brain into thinking it's an actual experience. It really is almost like being there.

Meditate On Love and Kindness

Science suggests that compassion may have a profound, evolutionary purpose because we humans have mirror neurons that react to other people's emotions and trigger in us a desire to help. Radiating compassion without discrimination makes you stronger and more resilient and instills greater happiness. The following meditation guides you from celebrating loving-kindness toward yourself, to celebrating four other people, then to all beings.

1. Use a breathing technique to induce a calm, centered state of mind.
2. Offer a prayer such as, *I dedicate the virtues of myself for the benefit of all.*
3. Think of four people to whom you will send love and then formulate an affirmation to help you arouse loving-kindness in your heart: *I am wanted and loved. I forgive myself and others. I feel my heart full of love. I hold in my heart the peace of the Divine. My loves call forth love, peace, and joy in all hearts.*
4. Feel the loving-kindness toward yourself.
5. Visualize each of the four people. Think of them swaddled in love, peace, and happiness as you radiate those feelings to them.
6. Think of the four directions the wind blows and then radiate love in all directions to beings of all spheres and realms.

Feel the Energy of Your Words

A big part of living a fearless and happy life is learning how to communicate effectively. Mantras teach you how to become more energy-focused in your communication, rather than word-focused. Sure, words have energy, but just because you hear words that have low vibrations (e.g., "This sucks!") doesn't mean you have to react to them. Notice the energy without judgment.

Rather than focusing on the meaning of the word, observe the energy and say, *I am learning to communicate in peaceful and empowering ways.* For example, if someone says "This sucks," observing the energy gives you information (guidance) that this person may feel overwhelmed or stuck in a situation. Then you can respond with, "Sounds like you feel stuck." This response is a much more effective way to free them than if you attempt to fix their issue or take on their frustration yourself.

✦

Follow your bliss
and don't be afraid,
and doors will
open where you
didn't know they
were going to be.

—JOSEPH CAMPBELL
American professor and author

Quiet Your Mind

Feeling stressed, overwhelmed, and decidedly unhappy? Try cooling down with this mini-meditation:

1. Stop whatever you are doing right now, close your eyes, and focus on your breath until your mind quiets.
2. As thoughts come up, allow them to float away by gently redirecting your mind back to your inhalations and exhalations, blotting out whatever is going on around you.
3. Stay in your mini-meditation for fifteen minutes (or start with five minutes and work your way up to fifteen minutes).

With practice, you can easily learn to quiet any mind chatter that may be distracting you. Doing a mini-meditation is a great way to refocus yourself and find some calm.

Do the Unexpected

If you want to feel alive and happy, get a little crazy. Do something spontaneous such as having a picnic (even in the front yard) or doing a totally out-of-the-ordinary activity like dancing under the light of the full moon or lying on fresh powder and making a snow angel. Maybe you take a day off and visit an architectural salvage yard, spend an afternoon antiquing, or take the subway to the end of the line just because you can. If it's springtime, go buy a packet of seeds for a butterfly garden and scatter them in a raked bed. If it's fall, make a pumpkin pie from scratch using a sugar pumpkin you buy at the farmers' market.

Whatever is out of the ordinary for you, give it a shot. You'll find youthful exuberance taking over and replacing the humdrum routine that might be bogging down your days. Make it a weekly ritual to find this happiness again and do something spontaneous.

Look Past the Physical Pain

Living in pain, whether it's emotional or physical, can lead to random and sometimes impulsive thinking. Thoughts such as *I am in so much pain*, *My head is killing me*, *I feel exhausted*, and *I need aspirin* can weaken your overall well-being. Instead of saying these kinds of things to yourself and fostering negativity, say this mantra: *Raising my awareness transcends these sensations now*. Rather than focusing on the pain, put your attention on transcending your thoughts and words.

✦

Happiness is
not something you
postpone for the
future; it is something
you design for
the present.

—JIM ROHN
American motivational speaker

Establish a Gourmet Dinner Club

Orchestrate a dinner party for friends who like great-tasting food. If you have a lot of fun at that dinner, suggest that the group form a gourmet dinner club that regularly gets together on a rotating basis in each friend's home. Remind everyone that planning and preparing a gourmet meal or finding appropriate wine is not necessarily as difficult as one might imagine. Every day, the Food Network brings extraordinary chefs into your living room to show you how. Most of those chefs say it starts with fresh, wholesome ingredients and a few basic pantry staples. Wine merchants are happy to help you find the perfect wine accompaniment for your food selection.

Sharing food is about more than just eating and drinking; you are sharing meaningful and pleasurable moments of your life with friends who are important to you.

Draw Your Inner Critic

Everyone's got at least one mean voice inside their head. You know, the one who says things like, *What were you thinking? Maybe there's just something wrong with you. You really screwed that one up.*

Whenever you're feeling unhappy and deeply negative, pull back the curtain on your inner critic by drawing a picture of her or him. How old is she? Does she wear glasses? What kinds of clothes do you imagine her in?

If you can personify the voice, you can see that it's not you. Which means you'll give her a little less stock the next time she starts in on you.

Accept Responsibility for Your Actions

You can't be happy if you're hiding guilt or some other hidden emotion. You must be fully honest, both with yourself and others, to be happy. If you find yourself struggling to open up and tell the truth about a difficult subject, tell yourself, *I am willing and ready to take full responsibilities for my actions.*

As you recite this mantra, keep in mind your intention is not to admit fault but rather to restore trust and respect with another or yourself. Offering an apology is so much more than simply admitting your mistakes. A true apology gives you a way to free yourself from carrying the burden of guilt and disappointment. Sincere apologies have no alternative agenda, and are incredibly powerful energy tools for rebuilding trust and harmony.

◆

Happiness radiates like the fragrance from a flower and draws all good things toward you.

—MAHARISHI MAHESH YOGI
Indian guru

Put a Bamboo Plant in Your Kitchen

Put a lucky bamboo plant on your kitchen counter where it will happily enjoy some warmth. Even if you don't have a green thumb, you can successfully grow this plant. It doesn't need much light and will thrive in water (as long as the water is clean and kept at the same level). According to the ancient Chinese tradition of feng shui, the lucky bamboo (not actually a bamboo at all but a member of the *Dracaena* genus) creates harmony wherever it is placed. Its numerous long green leaves grow out of a single stalk. If you work from home, put a six-stalk plant in your office to attract prosperity or a three-stalk plant in the bedroom to ensure longevity, wealth, and happiness.

Forgive Old Hurts

The natural state of your true self is one of joy and rapture. Holding on to anger and pain toward someone you haven't been able to forgive for a hurt inflicted in the past only agitates your mental suffering; you feel angry, sad, confused, and less positive about life. Such feelings hamper your spiritual progress and can take a toll on your happiness. Conversely, forgiveness can bring you a healthier attitude, lower blood pressure, less hostility, and higher self-esteem and psychological well-being. Place the value of your good health over holding on to a grudge. Discuss your feelings with a trusted friend, listen to forgiveness tapes, or seek professional help, if necessary, but find a way to let go, forgive, and focus on the here and now. When you do, you create room in your heart and mind for peace to enter.

Stay Calm in a Traffic Jam

If you live in or around a major city, you know how difficult and frustrating traffic jams can be. You're not moving anywhere, everyone is angry, and loud horns are blaring all around. Block out the negative energy by telling yourself, *I hear joyful noises and feel love all around me.* Crank up some smooth jazz, melodic classical, or whatever your favorite genre of music is and transform those harsh horns into peaceful music.

✦

Be happy for this moment. This moment is your life.

—OMAR KHAYYAM
Persian poet

Drink Water

Staying hydrated gives you more energy, improves your skin's texture and color, and gives your body what it needs to function properly. Even mild dehydration can have cognitive effects on your mood, decrease your memory, and impact brain function. In fact, many people mistake symptoms of dehydration for symptoms of depression! If you are feeling lethargic, have difficulty concentrating, or have trouble remembering things, you may need to drink more water. When you get enough water, your body will feel healthier and happier.

✦

Even the
darkest night
will end
and the sun
will rise.

—VICTOR HUGO
French poet, author, and playwright

Index